Town T
Wincanto.

Living in Wincanton

A collection of memories

Recorded, transcribed and edited by

Jenny Peet

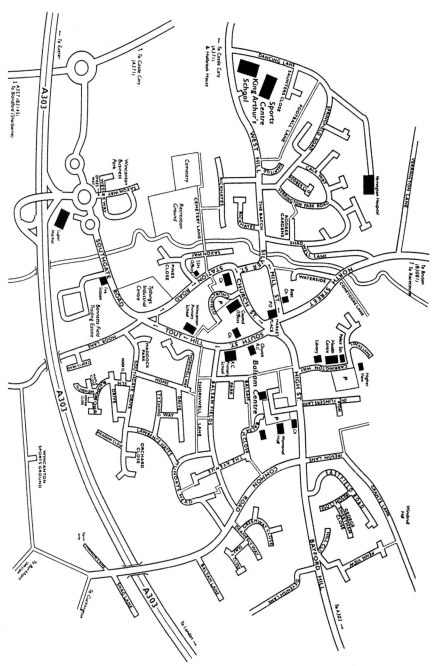

Wincanton – Queen of the Vale

By same author

Village Voices - Charlton Horethorne

First Published in 2006 by Tomorrow's History
Pippin Cottage
North Road
Charlton Horethorne
Sherborne
Dorset
DT9 4NS
peet.pippin@virgin.net

ISBN 0-9552430-1-7
978-0-9552430-1-1

Further copies of this book can be obtained from

Wincanton Museum
32 High Street
Wincanton
BA9 9JF

Wincanton Town Hall
Market Place
Wincanton
BA9 9LD
01963 31693

Chris Kemp
01963 31059

Printed by Remous Ltd., Milborne Port, Sherborne Dorset DT9 5EP

Acknowledgements

I would like to thank everyone who has assisted in the publication of this book, especially the following;-

The twenty participants who so willingly shared their memories and photographs.

Awards for All for the generous lottery grant to the Wincanton Museum.

The Wincanton Museum Trustees for all their support and for book sales.

Wincanton Town Hall for book sales.

Margaret Prettejohns for the cover photographs.

F.W.B. Printing, Wincanton for permission to use their town map.

All the proceeds from the sale of this book will go towards the upkeep and maintenance of Wincanton Museum for the benefit of future generations.

Contents

A Peculiar Thing to Swallow - Ruby Stevenson

I was born in 1918 at Glastonbury. My mother and father had moved from Kent for safety's sake with a Miss McKenzie at the beginning of the First World War. My father was her gardener and my mother already had five children and after I came along there were two more. Mother had her last baby when she was forty-four.

Father was a soldier in the First World War and after he came home on Christmas leave I was born the following September. In between time my mother had received her widow's papers, to say that father was dead, but she wouldn't sign them because she said she knew he was alive. As it happened she didn't get confirmation that he was alive until the August. He had been taken prisoner in the February and when he returned mother said he was never the same man.

Two years after dad came back we moved to East Lydford where he was a gardener at Lydford Hall for a Mrs Paulette. As a young man he had done his training at Bedsbury in Kent, which is now part of the Wisley gardens, so he grew fruit, flowers and vegetables and was also the handyman. There wasn't much he couldn't turn his hand to if need be.

Later we moved to Redlynch, near Bruton where dad was gardener and handyman at Redlynch House. We lived in a row of cottages where the butler, the groom and the cowman lived. It was when we lived there that I started school. I was five years old and every day I walked there, wearing good strong boots, with my brother who was ten. Two and a half miles it was to the school and at the end of the day we had to walk the same distance back home. I was in the infants' school, which was in the High Street in Bruton, and Arthur went to the senior school down by the packhorse bridge. Every dinnertime I crossed the road and walked down to the senior school to have my dinner with my brother - mostly jam sandwiches.

Next door to the senior school was a sweet shop and one day I had been given a ha'penny so I bought a stick of liquorice which had a balloon on the end. The balloons weren't made out of the same material then as they are now. Back at the Infants' school somebody told me that if I put the balloon in my mouth I could blow it up. I put the balloon in my mouth, took one gulp, and swallowed it! I remember it was a Friday. My brother was summoned to come up to the Infants' school to collect me and walk me back home with a note for mother. I recall Arthur hitting me all the way home because he was missing a lesson he'd been looking forward to. The note from the teacher telling what had happened was handed over to mother and it said would she give me a dose of castor oil and await results. This was Friday, and the result turned up on Monday morning. It was a bright pink balloon when I swallowed it but it was colourless on Monday morning!

When I was six, in 1924, we moved to Abergavveny Cottages, Lower Holbrook, Wincanton and my father worked at Suddon Grange. The cottage was one of a pair of semis and Mr Humphries, next door, was the lorry driver, van driver and chauffeur for Mr Vesey of Suddon Grange. There were seven of us children at the time, my youngest brother hadn't been born, and we had to manage with three small bedrooms. My eldest sister had epileptic fits, something to do with her being frightened by a Great Dane dog, and she died when I was sixteen. Because of that mother and father very seldom went out together.

The washing was done every Monday morning. Water was collected from outside and carried in heavy galvanised steel buckets and poured into the copper which was in a lean-to at the back of the house. The copper was built out of bricks and was square and in the middle was a big iron bowl. Underneath this you lit a fire to boil the water. The sheets and towels were always boiled, so they went straight into the copper. Anything else was washed by hand in an enamel basin with hot water from the copper.

There was no sink in the house. We had to wash in the enamel bowl and once a week we carried a big tin bath into the house, set it in front of the fire, carried the hot water in from the copper and had a bath. Kettles had to be boiled on the open fire.

We had a big black range and if possible we had a roast of some description every Sunday, which was cooked in the range oven. Mother always did her baking on a Sunday morning because she had the fire going for the roast meat. She made pastry, jam tarts and treacle tarts nearly every week and sometimes she made small cakes but she never made a big cake. Meat was kept cool in a meat safe, which hung on a nail on the outside wall of the scullery, and had zinc mesh on the front to keep out flies.

The lavatory was at the end of the garden and if you needed to go when it was dark you took the paraffin hurricane lantern. The contents landed in a bucket and when it was getting full we dug a hole in the garden and buried it. That was dad's job. We also kept a bucket in the scullery which we used to wee in instead of going outside.

In 1929 Mr and Mrs Vesey lost all their money on the Wall Street Crash. Mrs Vesey was American and came from Boston. Before that time they employed two gardeners, a groom, a cowman, three dairy maids, a cook, a housemaid, a parlour maid and the other gardener's wife used to help with the rough work in the house. They had a lot of land and ran a big herd of Guernsey cows and they had to get rid of all that. In the end only dad and the groom, Wilfred Dunstan, and the woman who used to go in and do the cleaning were kept on. All the rest had to go. Mrs Vesey had to learn how to cook!

My school days were not normal. Just after I started infant school I had an eye test and they discovered that I was very short sighted. I wore a patch over one eye to strengthen the other. I was not allowed to write on paper or read much from a book. When the other girls did sewing I couldn't do that either so I knitted. I did all my lessons in the corner of the classroom on a blackboard and easel, so that I could write large letters with chalk. When we had exams I went in a classroom on my own, with my blackboard and easel and one schoolteacher, so the other pupils could not copy what I was writing. I wasn't supposed to read at home in the evenings, but I did, and I've been a reader all my life.

I left school, and home, at fourteen and went to work for the manager of the Westminster Bank in Wincanton as a general maid. I lived in and got up at seven o'clock in the morning. I had to light the kitchen stove, prepare a full cooked breakfast for two, make sure the dining room was clean and tidy and the fire was burning - all before they sat down to breakfast at eight o'clock. Mrs Lake had had many maids before me, I don't know how many, and she also had several after.

Each Monday Mrs Lake did her grocery ordering and one Monday she gave me a jar of jam which had enough in the bottom for just one slice of bread. During the day she made some rock cakes, and I was allowed to have one, and when I was having my tea she walked through the kitchen and she said to me, 'By the way, Ruby, when you have jam for tea you can't have cake.' I wasn't allowed to have jam on a slice of bread and a rock cake.

Every night I took my clock into her room for her to wind up and set the alarm. One morning she came down to breakfast and the dining room fire wasn't burning and she turned round and told me off about it. I told her if she wanted it done she had to damned well do it herself! I had only been there for three weeks. She stood at the open dining room door and shouted to her husband, 'Dick, did you hear? She swore at me.' Then she turned to me and said, 'Go and pack your bags at once.' So I did and went home with a note to my father, and twenty-one shillings for three weeks' work, explaining why I had got the sack. He wasn't a very happy man.

I was home about a week. At that time Wincanton had a laundry and mother suggested I apply for a job there. They took me on and I was there for twelve and a half years before I got married. I sorted the dirty laundry, marked it, sent it for washing and then packed it when it was clean.

Sorting the laundry was a very unpleasant job. You often had some filthy articles and we had a family who lived in one of the villages who sent laundry in and when it arrived it was hopping with fleas. We had to take it into the corner of the sorting room to deal with and afterwards we checked our ankle socks to kill any fleas that

Wincanton laundry taken from the top of the Cow and Gate chimney

had lodged in them. We had everything come to the laundry. Some things came in a filthy condition. We also washed sanitary towels which went into a special washing machine. During the war we did laundry for both British and American soldiers. The American's laundry was only from the officers, ladies and gentlemen, and sometimes in the gentlemen's pockets you would find a certain rubber article. We had to bundle that back up for returning with a label saying, 'Sorry, but we do not wash rubber articles.'

When I was seventeen I left home and went to live with some friends who lived closer to the laundry. One night we went to a dance in Castle Cary, just a few of us, boys and girls, and there was hardly anyone there so we spent the evening in the bar. They were feeding me on port and whisky and I can remember saying, 'I couldn't walk across that room if you paid me.' Evidently I passed out. I can remember them giving me coffee and sticking their fingers down my throat to try to make me sick, which didn't work. This was Thursday. On the Friday I didn't go to work. On Monday morning I got reprimanded and sent to the manageress's office. She tore a strip off me because I had been incapable of going to work on the Friday because I was drunk the night before. I have never drunk port since and it is within only the last eight years that I can face whisky.

In 1945 I met a Scotsman who was in the army and was stationed at Dimmer Camp, near Castle Cary. A corporal from the camp came into the laundry and said they were having a dance the following Saturday to celebrate the end of the war in Europe and would any of us girls like to go. We said yes, and hired a taxi, and went to the Constitutional Hall in Castle Cary where I met my husband to be, David, or Jock as he was called. I remember drinking gin in tumblers. I was wearing a pink crepe dress which shrunk when it got wet. Somebody spilt some beer down it and where it was wet it shrunk above my knee.

The following Tuesday the corporal brought in a note to the laundry to say that Jock would like to meet me so I arranged to meet him under the Wincanton Town Clock on the Saturday night. He didn't turn up. When the corporal came back the following Tuesday he brought me in a letter from Jock to say that he was sorry he hadn't turned up but he had been put on guard duty. Would I make another date? I did and we married in January 1946.

When Jock was de-mobbed we went to Scotland and lived with his mother in an upstairs flat. His step-sister and her husband and two babies were in one bedroom, me and Jock in the other bedroom, and his mother slept in the sitting room. Only a few months afterwards his mother had a stroke and died. I didn't know a soul and was a stranger in a strange land and the English weren't looked on all that well in those days. If something special came into the baker's shop other people got it, I didn't. The day after Jock's mother died we had a letter come from the City Factor, because it was a council flat, to say that we all had to get out because mother was the tenant and we weren't. Jock and I went to see him and asked if we moved out would they let his step-sister and husband and children have the flat. He said yes, providing we signed a document to say we wouldn't go back. We had to find somewhere else to live.

We found a Mrs Robertson round the corner who had a three bedroom parlour house - a kitchen, living room and sitting room. She let us have an upstairs bedroom for seven shillings and sixpence a week. I was allowed to do my washing on a Thursday afternoon and I was supposed to have use of the kitchen as well. On a Sunday if I didn't get down in the kitchen before half past nine I couldn't get in there until half past four in the afternoon. We had an open fire in our bedroom and a walk in wardrobe which contained a tea chest. The coal man used to come upstairs and tip the coal in the tea chest and I cooked, more often than not, on the open fire with a saucepan.

It was whilst we were living in this house that I became pregnant. When Donald was born Mrs Robertson wrote and told my mother that she would look after me like her own daughter. The Monday afternoon I came home with Donald, my husband only had two hours off work to pick me up and take me home, I found that Mr and Mrs Robertson had gone to the pictures for the afternoon. Talk about looking after me as a daughter!

By this time my mother in Wincanton had moved into the house adjoining the one I lived in as a child, and my sister lived in the one we had lived in as a family. Mother wrote to us in Dundee and told us that sister Grace had been allocated a council house in Wincanton so the house next door would be empty. The owners said we could take over that cottage so in 1948 we moved back to Lower Holbrook. We were delighted, my husband got a job at Wincanton Transport, and after eight and a half years we were given a council house.

Transporting Cattle - Jack Collard

I was born in 1918 in Leigh Common in the parish of Penselwood which is a couple of miles out of Wincanton. My father was Edgar and my mother was Doris Sweetman. Her father was a farmer and her uncle was George Sweetman, the local historian. There were three of us children in the family.

My father was a cattle dealer and farmer, as was his father before him. His customers were the local farmers who didn't have time to go and buy their own cattle because they were too busy. In my father's day he bought cattle locally from Salisbury, Dorchester, Yeovil and Shaftsbury markets which were held fortnightly. He also went to annual fairs - the one at Wareham was held in the Spring and it was said that farmers returning home would bring back the cuckoo! If he was going to Salisbury he took the pony and trap to Gillingham station and then caught the train to Salisbury - and he could do it as quickly then as you can do it by car today. The cattle he bought were loaded onto the train to bring back here to Wincanton.

Every so often my father went to the Bristol market to buy Irish cattle which were shipped over to Bristol by boat. They would be walked from the docks through the City to the market, which was below Temple Meads station, where they would be loaded onto the train and delivered to Wincanton and walked from the station to the farm.

There was no telephone at the farm. A boy on a bicycle with a pork pie hat delivered a telegram from Wincanton Post office telling us that a cattle boat would be docking in Bristol at such and such a time. This method of communication from the auctioneers contin-ued right through to the 1950s.

On Saturdays, as a boy, I helped with the delivering of dairy cattle to the farmers in the villages around. The most popular breed in those days was Shorthorns. We would put the calves in a horse drawn cart and the heifers followed behind on foot. I helped to drive them and we walked all the way to Stourton, unloaded the animals and collected the ones that were being replaced (cast cows) and then walked all the way back home to Wincanton. We even drove the cattle to Shaftsbury market by foot. Father never drove any cattle because we had four drovers who worked for us. The market was on a Thursday, so two days before we drove them just past half way to Shaftsbury, near Gillingham, where they were put in a field and rested overnight. We then came home by pony and trap and returned early the next morning to continue driving the animals to the market. The cast cows were either sent to Shepton Mallet market or to a meat wholesaler in Birmingham by train.

Father also had a customer for dairy cattle in London. The cows were sent by train to the city where they were kept in stalls at the Elephant and Castle. This was in the 1920s when milkmen used a horse and cart to sell milk from churns in residential areas.

Just after the war the government decided to go ahead with the eradication of tuberculosis in cattle and those cattle which failed the test, the reactors, were destroyed. In Scotland the farmers, veterinary surgeons and auctioneers had anticipated this and were in a position to supply the large number of cattle needed by the English farmers to replace the reactors. From 1949 to the 1970s onwards I travelled to Scotland every two weeks to buy Ayrshires. I caught the Pines Express, which was a train that ran from Bournemouth to the Midlands - Birmingham, Manchester, Crewe and Liverpool. The train stopped at Wincanton every day, at my request, at about 11 o'clock and after changing trains at Crewe and I could be in the south of Scotland at around 6-7 o'clock in the evening.

The next day I would attend the market, or visit farmers to buy the animals. The cattle were loaded on the train at about 4 o'clock in the afternoon and unloaded in Wincanton the following day and delivered to my customers by cattle lorry. Dr Beeching, the Government advisor, then came on the scene and closed down a lot of railway lines so I had to change my travel plans and fly up to Scotland from Heathrow. When the local railway line closed the cattle had to be collected from Bath by lorry. Later, when the M6 was opened, they were transported all the way from Scotland by lorry. Many people complained about the railway line being closed but I was often the only person on the train.

Fog was the biggest problem in the winter time. One particular December I boarded the night sleeper to come back from Scotland. The train was due into London Euston station at about 7 o'clock in the morning but we didn't arrive until 2 o'clock in the afternoon. I went to the hotel next to the station to have lunch and you couldn't see across the dining room because the fog was so thick. Many people were walking around with masks on and the taxis had youngsters running in front of them with burning torches so they could be seen. On the same day a number of cows at Smithfield fat-stock show died because they couldn't breathe properly. That particular day was the worst they ever had for fog.

Snow sometimes held up the train for two or three hours but it wasn't a real problem. If there was any delay in the service, outside Birmingham at Snow Hill, there were cattle pens where the animals could be fed and watered and then loaded back on for the rest of the journey. At the end of the journey the cattle trucks were sent from Wincanton to a siding just north of Bath where they were mucked out, washed and cleaned ready to be used again.

The largest auction I attended in Scotland had 1581 cows which were sold in a three day sale. In the mid fifties I was asked to be one of the judges at a Scottish show and I continued to judge cattle for many years. I was also asked to judge cattle locally from time to time. Once a year I had a sale of my own cattle, the last one being in 1970.

Jack on the right presenting the cup for the Champion Heiffer,
Pedigree Show and Sale, Castle Douglas, Scotland.

I remember the first car we had, a Model T Ford, known as a Ford Tin Lizzie. There were no models in those days…..and they were all black! Father never drove a car in his life, he preferred his pony and trap, but we had a man who did. He drove father round all the farms in the area to buy cattle. We had an outing one day to Porlock and to go up Porlock Hill we had to turn the car round and go up in reverse because we couldn't go up in first gear. I passed my driving test in 1936 when I was eighteen years old.

The most enjoyable events in those days were the Hunt Balls. The best one was held at Inwood House in Templecombe which was owned by the local female squire, Miss Guest. She had her own hunt which was known as Miss Guest's Hunt. In the thirties there were loads of different hunts in the area and nearly each one had its own Ball. The Hunt Ball was a very special occasion. The men wore black ties, now we call them bow ties, but in those days you had to tie your own bow. Miss Guest would wear hunting pink, the red jacket of the huntsman, and some of the other huntsmen did as well. All the ladies had ball gowns - my wife had quite a few of them.

The buffet supper was served by maids, watched over by the butler. We had top notch dance bands like the Showering's band from Shepton Mallet. I remember going all the way to the South and West Wiltshire hunt ball once. Anyone could go to a hunt ball, you didn't have to be a huntsman. To belong to a meeting you didn't have to wait for an invitation, you just turned up on your horse and joined in. A large number of riders would be there, anything up to fifty. It was very popular and you could hunt every week in the season which ran from January to March. Another occasion we looked forward to was the annual police ball.

We were married sixty-five years ago during the war in 1940, at West Stour, and went on our honeymoon to Penzance. When we got to Yeovil to catch the train the siren was blowing the 'all clear' following a bombing raid. Arriving in Penzance the following day we saw everybody looking out to sea - they'd had their first bombs dropped.

We have two children and four grandchildren and all I do now is enjoy our nine great grand children. My great granddaughter recently went to a party in the school in Penselwood, the very same school that I attended all those years ago.

The Pills were Hand Made - Mary Dyke

I was born in 1920 and had two brothers, one older and one younger. My father was the eldest boy of nine, from Wiveliscombe, and he went to Bristol to learn the baking trade. My mother, who was born near Wellington, was the eldest girl of nineteen children, and was in service with a Doctor and his family in Wiveslicombe. My parents married in 1913 and bought a bakery in Somerton where they worked long hours and gradually built up the business.

The dough for the bread was mixed by hand to start with, and mother made all the jam for the cakes. Later a mixing machine was bought which was driven by petrol and then in 1931 an electric one was purchased. Originally the bread was delivered by horse and cart. The horse, whose name was Kit, was kept in a stable in the field at the back of the house and catching it to put on the harness was quite a business. Later we had two delivery vans, with drivers, and my two brothers also worked in the business.

Every Saturday night I enjoyed a bath in a galvanised tub in the bakehouse which was always warm from the heat of the coke fuelled ovens and where there was a hot water tap. At Christmas time when the bakehouse was closed, because the ovens were hot, friends and neighbours brought round their chickens and father cooked them free of charge.

Mary right, with brothers Frederic and John.

Because my parents worked so hard there was enough money to send me to board at Barnstaple Grammar School. My mother took me by train to Taunton and then put me on the Barnstaple one. My Auntie May lived in Barnstaple and was able to do my washing which I took round to her on Saturday mornings. There were 22 girls living in a big house, run by two mistresses, which was three quarters of a mile away from the school. We had to walk there each day, summer and winter alike, through the park by the river. The three dormitories had no heat but there was hot water in the bathrooms. The fire was lit in the evenings in the lounge where we had prayers before going to bed.

The uniform was a brown gymslip, black stockings and shoes, blazer and in the winter we wore a gaberdine mac. We wore Panama hats in the summer and in the winter a thick felt hat with a brim, you were never allowed out in your uniform without your hat! These were not my happiest days, I was homesick, but I did enjoy playing tennis and hockey.

In 1936 I started work at Bonds the Chemist, next door to where I lived in Somerton. In those days the prescriptions were written in Latin and medicines were mixed in bottles, which I had to wash. The ingredients were measured on little scales and mixed with water. We made our own pills. First of all I would crush all the ingredients in a pestle and mortar and add some liquid to bind it all together into a small ball. I then flattened it out and ran over it with a grooved board which cut it up into little portions. Each portion was then rolled by hand into a pill, wrapped in a small square of white paper, sealed with sealing wax and labelled. I worked from nine in the morning until seven at night with a half day on Wednesday when I usually played tennis on a grass court, or badminton in winter. I loved my sport.

In September 1942, when I was working at Timothy White's in

Yeovil, I had a phone message at 9.15am to tell me that the Somerton milk factory had been bombed and eleven people had been killed. Luckily my fiancé Don, who worked in the laboratory and was exempt from the forces, had a miraculous escape suffering only a shattered ear drum. The surviving employees were sent to either the Totnes or the Wincanton Cow and Gate factory. Don was sent to Wincanton, and we married in the December. After four days honeymoon in London in the blackout we moved to Wincanton where we lived in lodgings with Mrs Cross in Balsam Park. There was another lodger living there as well so my husband and I had one bedroom, the other lodger had another and we shared a bathroom and Mrs Cross did all the cooking. I was able to get a job in the Dried Milk Products office at Cow and Gate where Don, of course, worked in the laboratory. On our day off we cycled back to Somerton, seventeen miles away to visit the family.

In 1944 I was expecting my first child and because I wasn't very well I went home to Somerton to live with my parents. In 1947 Don and I were given a council flat in Rickhayes, and Susan, our second daughter, was born at Templecombe Hospital. In 1954 we bought 3 Laburnam Villas from Cow and Gate and in 1960 our third daughter was born at Templecome.

I have now lived in Wincanton for over sixty years and look back fondly on many happy memories.

The Workhouse, Medals and Rabbit Fur - William Rumbold

I was born at 3, Whitehall, Wincanton in 1921 which was at the bottom of the hill leading to the racecourse, and lived there for fourteen years. My father died in 1921, the year in which I was born, and my mother was left with three boys to bring up. Father had been shell shocked and gassed during the First World War at the battle of Mons. Robert, my oldest brother went to live with my grandparents up the road at 9 Whitehall.

Nearby was Shadwell Shoot. When the railway was built there were lots of springs in the hills. The land needed to be drained, and they had to collect the water somehow, so the railway company piped it down into the bottom of the town so it could be used by people in the surrounding cottages.

I have a very vivid memory of climbing up onto a chair, opening a drawer and picking up a blue bottle of camphorated oil. I was three years old. I can see myself doing it now! I had a good old mouthful and I don't remember anything more - it had knocked me out! My mother rushed up to the doctor's house, which was where the convent School is now in South Street, with me out cold in her arms. Apparently Dr Coulson said, 'Put him down there. If he comes to he will be all right.'

The Board of Guardians met at the Workhouse in Shadwell Lane. Mr Roberts was the Master of the Workhouse and the Guardians held their meetings in a big room attached to the main house. I remember going there with my mother, looking inside the room and seeing a massive mahogany table around which they were all sitting. Mother had gone to see if the Parish could grant her two shillings a week. Anyway she went in and I had to sit outside on a wooden bench in the corridor. One man thought my mother was a needy case, Farmer Candy from Pensel Wood, but nobody else agreed so she came out empty handed.

Mother had a pension from the government for us three boys and herself of ten shillings a week. The rent for the cottage was four shillings and sixpence so she took in washing to make ends meet, charging four pence per hour. There were two Miss Rogers and they lived in a house on Bayford Hill, right at the top of the town, and one of my jobs was to walk all the way up there to collect their dirty washing in a clothes basket. Mother washed and ironed it and I took it back to them. It was nearly always two shillings and three pence ha'penny. The maid would bring out the money and I had to sign the book to say I had received it and I got right proficient, scribbling, 'With thanks.'

In the cottage there were two rooms downstairs and two bedrooms upstairs and you had to go through one bedroom to get into the other. The floor in the first bedroom fell off a bit, was sloping, so there had to be some blocks under the bed to bring it up level. The back room downstairs was a bit like a kitchen. The copper was in there to boil water and there was a range for mother to cook on. Caraway cakes were one of our favourites, and they were cooked in the oven at the side of the range. If it got burnt on the outside you just scraped a bit of it off. Pans of soup and vegetables were pushed into the open fire to cook. I remember the Doctor calling one day, when my mother was dishing out our dinner onto the plates, and she simply opened the drawers of the kitchen cupboard and pushed the plates in out of sight so that the kitchen looked nice and tidy.

Mother did the decorating inside the house. She mixed flour paste with which to hang the wallpaper. In the front bedroom there was a chimney breast which went diagonally across the wall. On the flat walls the pattern would be upright but on the chimney breast my mother hung it to follow the angle of the chimney.

Outside we had one tap which served three houses and one outside lavatory for the same three houses. There was no flush, you had to throw a bucket of water down. I don't remember there being any problems, or anybody shouting, 'come on'. I would go outside every morning before school to have a wash under the tap, with just my trousers on; summer or winter, it made no difference. I'd wash my hair and face, and our next door neighbour, whom we called Granny Sweet, reckoned if I carried on doing that I would die. She was a dear old soul.

Eight yards from our back door was the River Cale and every so often Jim and I went fishing with jam jars. We kept minnows in jars for so long and then threw them back. I remember standing fishing on the river bank and the next thing I knew I would be feet first in the water. I was sort of mesmerised.

We had a garden on the other side of the road which belonged to Mr Pitman who had a shoe shop in Wincanton. We paid ten shillings a year for its use and grew potatoes, cabbages, parsnips and lots of different vegetables. Jim and I looked after it mostly when we got a bit older. A packet of seeds in those days had lots in. Now you have a job to feel if there are any in the packet at all.

She was very clever, was my mother. In 1926, when it was carnival time, she got a piece of old sacking and sewed a lot of spent matches onto it which I then wore with a sign saying, 'No More Strikes,' - this was the time of the miner's strikes. On another occasion she bought some cast iron blue wheels from Billy English, and made up a frame to look like a big boot so it became The Old Woman Who Lived in a Shoe. Mother dressed up as the Old Woman and dolls were children in the shoe. In those days there was a carnival procession in the afternoon and another in the evening and they always took the same route. Some town folks didn't like it - you always get some folk who are not prepared to do anything themselves but crib at those that have a go. When we reached the age of around twelve years we were each given a broom handle with a tin on the top with a piece of wick in, torches to illuminate the parade, and stood along the route of the carnival. For doing that we were paid six pence.

William, 3rd from left, and friends

In the same year, just after the miner's strike, a miner came down to Whitehall. He had a single-breasted mac on, a flat cap and a string of three medals from the First World War, which were known as Pip, Squeak and Wilfred. He had probably walked from Midsomer Norton or Radstock where a lot of miners lived. They were starving, they had absolutely nothing, no dole money, nothing and in the end they went back to work for less money than they had gone out on strike for. That was a dirty trick to play on the coal miners. Times weren't too bright then. He stood outside our house and sang to raise a bit of money. Mother handed some over to me and my brother Jim, and we had to decide which one of us was going to go out and give him two pence for singing to us. I don't recall which one of us did. I fancy we both went out in the end. We also had a gentleman of the road call regularly for some boiling water so that he could make some tea. That's all he wanted, boiling water, and he was no trouble.

My grandfather always described himself as, 'A dealer in precious metals and furs.' He collected lead and copper and brass and rabbit skins. He was a rag and bone man! At the back of his cottage was a big shed where everything was stored until it was collected, which was about once a week. A firm from Yeovil came to collect the metal but I can't remember who took the rabbit skins. Grandpa Jim couldn't write his name so he used to put his cross in a special fashion. He bought ten boxes of bloaters at a time, no money ever changed hands, and when somebody came out with a few rags, skins or a bit of metal he would tell them how many bloaters it was worth. He travelled as far out as Charlton Musgrove.

Grandfather was a clever old poacher and you could buy a rabbit off him for sixpence and if you let him have the skin back he would give you a penny for it. We would eat one rabbit a week, which would be either stewed or roasted. We took it in turns to eat the different joints, if I ate the back leg, Jim ate what was on its back. The following week Jim would have the back leg and I would have the back meat. When he was over eighty years old grandfather could still be seen pushing his hand-cart around the town. If we boys were hungry we went up to his cottage and kept on at him until he gave us a bloater to eat. We wrapped the fish up in a bit of newspaper, the Sunday People I think it was, and made a space in the fire grate and put the bloater parcel in the fire. When the paper was burnt it was cooked a treat.

In 1937 came the Slum Clearance Act and our cottages at Whitehall were declared slums. By this time Granny had died, and when it came time to clear out the houses, my grandfather said he wasn't going to move anywhere, he was staying right where he was. So they knocked down cottages numbers one to eight and ten to twenty one and Grandpa Jim continued to live in number nine. Eventually he knew he had to go but he stuck out for long enough, he was a tough old chap.

At School - For Seventy Eight Years - Sylvia Pleasants

I was born in 1923 just up the road, here in South Street, at Life Guard Villas opposite the school and moved into this house when I got married in 1947. In fact I've lived in this street all my life. I was one of twins but my sister died when she was two years old. Then my mother had a little boy when I was seven years old but he died when he was only eight. Mum lost dad at the age of fifty seven, from cancer, after she had nursed him at home for two years. When I look back now I realise what a sad life she had.

Sylvia, 2 years old

My parents came from Shepton Mallet. My father went to the Great War where he was wounded. He had a bullet go right through his head, in through the back and out through the front, and his arm was wounded as well which left him with a funny shaped wrist. Although you could clearly see where the bullet had gone through his head it hadn't affected him in any way. I remember him talking about being in the trenches and the problems with frostbite and how they used to soak their feet in urine to try to prevent it. When he was discharged from the army he saw an advert for a postman in Wincanton. He got the job and travelled to work by train from Shepton Mallet. When he was delivering the post he saw that the Life Guard Villas house was for rent, my parents got married, and that is how they came to live in Wincanton. He was quite a clever man and would go on conferences for the post office.

My mother left school when she was thirteen and was packed off to service in Shepton Mallet and then on to West Pennard. She worked first as a kitchen maid and then became a cook. I never heard her say a bad word about any of her employers - she always said to her it was a home and a roof over her head.

There was an old turnpike down the road here which was split into two cottages. In one cottage lived Miss Roper who was a very skilled dressmaker who also sold materials. Next door lived her brother who was a chimney sweep. Behind my house here was the orchard and at the bottom of the street the old fire station. Across the road where the school lay-by is now was a lodging house and an old cottage. Miss Jacobs lived there and she kept a pony and trap. Opposite Life Guard Villas is the school which I attended. Who was generally last at getting to school…..me!

The school had infants in the middle, girls at one end and boys at the other. The boys had the front playground and the girls had a playground further round. We were even taught separately, but we made eyes at the boys as we walked past. The children from the outlying villages who didn't have time to go home for their dinners

Exercises in the school yard. Sylvia on the right with the white shoes

brought sandwiches. To eat them they were locked in the classroom until they had finished, along with a teacher of course. My father on his rounds as a postman got to know a family whose little girl hated being locked in, so for years she came across the road to us where my mum fed her dinner all her school days. There were quite a number of poor children in the school because there was a chil- drens' home in North Street and another in Rodber House.

When we reached the age of eleven we all had to take the eleven plus examination. The year that I took it no-one in the school passed. But this wasn't because we weren't clever enough, it was because there were not enough places at the Grammar School for the number of children taking the exam. So I stayed at the same school until I was fourteen.

During the war I worked at Cow and Gate in the office as a confi- dential secretary and because my job was classed as being as a job of national importance I didn't have to go away. I started work at 8.30am, went home for lunch, and then worked through to 6pm, or later if I couldn't balance the books. After a bit of a break I walked down to Rockhill House in North Street where I manned the switchboard several nights a week on Air Raid Patrol duty. If any emergencies came in, such as fires or enemy aircraft flying near, I would have to alert whoever was needed. I walked all the way home in the blackout at midnight, there were strange soldiers all about the town who were billeted here, and I never felt frightened. At the weekends the office staff at Cow and Gate were expected to go into the factory to help on the packing lines, all for the love of it, to ensure the dried milk was ready for distribution. The day the bomb dropped on the bank in Wincanton I didn't know a thing about it until my father returned from his postman's round - I had been fast asleep and had never heard a thing!

During the war we had National Savings Weeks and it was one of my jobs to go around the houses selling savings stamps for the war effort. After the war the school decided it would start a Savings Bank for the pupils to learn how to save money and as I had experience of collecting I was asked to run it for them. The children brought in money and I would enter the amount on special cards and then when they had saved a certain amount it would be transferred to their own National Savings Bank books. When they wanted to withdraw some money they would have to go up to the Post Office.

Over the years I have continued to be involved in the school. I was Clerk to the Governors for 21 years and was made an Honorary Freeman of the School in December 1992. From time to time I take a few old toys over and have a lovely time trying to explain to the children what life was like when I was growing up, here, in Wincanton.

No Time to Dig Latrines -Theo Shave

I was born in Ringwood, Hampshire in 1924, where my father was a butcher. Unfortunately he went bankrupt and we came to Wincanton to live and dad worked for Bartlett's butchers. When we moved here there were three children but eventually there were eight of us, and I'm the eldest.

I went to school in Wincanton and left to work at the Cow and Gate factory where I tested the baby food to make sure it wasn't contaminated. I was called up to serve in the Army in 1942 but failed the medical, and I never knew why. However, I was called up again in January 1944. Eighteen year olds then were different to eighteen year olds now. We didn't travel much like they do today, we were naïve, in fact the furthest I had ever travelled was to places like Bournemouth, Salisbury, and Weymouth. To join the army would give me the opportunity to travel. I wasn't worried about fighting, at that age you don't have fear. I thought it was just a job and even when we were fighting the Japanese I thought that.

I went to Colchester where we did five weeks at the General Service School where we were drilled and licked into shape. I came home for a weeks leave and then went to Mudesley on Sea in Norfolk for intensive training. For six weeks we learned how to use a bayonet, how to fire a rifle and how to clear houses. I thought we were being prepared for the Normandy landings but after a fortnights leave we were issued with tropical kit so we knew we were either going to the Middle East, Egypt or India. Within two weeks of returning from leave we were on a boat from Scotland bound for India.

Funnily enough before I was called up I was helping a man over at Bayford called Sid Godfrey who had a small garage out there and he said to me, 'In six months the war will be over.' When I got called up I was told, 'Oh, you'll be all right. After your six months training it will be over.' When I knew that I was going abroad I was told, 'By the time you've got acclimatised it will be over.' Where I went it went on for another six years!

Theo in Burma

We arrived in Bombay to find everything totally different to England. The local people were either filthy rich or filthy poor. Nowadays when we switch on the television we see so many starving people so, to some extent, you get used to it. Then it was different and for the first time we saw people living on the streets in abject poverty. It was a dreadful shock to see them, and to see how they were treated by some of the British who had been in India for some time. They were the white Sahibs, they thought they were the rulers, and they treated the poor terrible. They'd throw stones at them sometimes or give them a clip round the ear and I used to say to some of the chaps, 'Why did you do that?' The answer always was, 'If you had lived out here as long as I have you'd know the reason why.'

We were sent to a transit camp called Doolally where we stayed for a few weeks to acclimatise and to train in the jungle. The food was atrocious. When I go to army camps now and see the way they live I have to say they lead a life of luxury compared with what we had. We each had a mess tin and had to form a long queue to collect our food. Breakfast was rice, plain boiled rice, and maybe fried bread and an egg. Tiffin time, that was lunch time, was soup and dinner was a bit of curry with hardly any meat in. As you queued you had to be on your guard against great big birds, eagles I think they were, which flew overhead ready to swoop down and grab whatever they could from your mess tins.

After a time we were put on a Dakota aeroplane and flown into Burma, to Kohema and Impual where the big battles had taken place. We were prepared for the big push down through the country, to drive out the Japanese, and were part of the 14th Army. My division was the 19th Indian Dagger Division, the most famous division that entered Burma, and my Battalion was the 2nd battalion of the Royal Berkshire Regiment.

When we were told that we were on the move to start sorting out the Japanese I hadn't been to the toilet for about five or six days. But that was the best dose of salts I ever had! If the company commander had known I would have been put on a charge because you were not allowed to be constipated. There were no toilets and there was no time to dig latrines, unless we had a two or three day rest period, so it was just a matter of going into the jungle. I've seen men with dysentery who have had to drop their trousers every five minutes - it was awful. And there was no such thing as toilet paper.

You were told not to drink water from wells, even if your tongue swelled up, because the Japanese contaminated them by dropping bodies down. But believe me, I pushed scum off pond water before drinking deeply. If you were caught drinking from your bottle, without the order being given, you would be put on a charge because water was scarce.

In those first few days in Burma many a time I had a clout around the ear by a chap called Lancaster, who used to look after me. He was an old timer and if I moved a stone with my hand there would be a bang across my ear hole. Because of scorpions you always had to use your boot to turn a stone. If you were stung by one of those you'd be out for a week, if you survived.

We wore long trousers with puttees, because of leeches. Your body was always moist, because of the heat, and if you scratched yourself it took ages and ages to heal. Then there were the snakes and mosquitoes to contend with. At night time you had to rub your face and the backs of your hands with something called Scat, to keep off the mosquitoes. The rest of your body was covered with your uniform, which you never took off, and for five months we were on the move all the time. Even your boots never came off. I was very fortunate in that I remained healthy. I took anti malaria tablets, salt tablets and anything that was going like vitamins or injections. A lot of the others didn't bother and became ill with things like jaundice, dysentery and prickly heat which is terrible if you get it under your armpits - it just feels like stinging nettles.

It wasn't long before I came across my first Japanese. I was on patrol looking out for the enemy in no man's land. Believe me, you didn't know the Japanese were there until you heard their machine guns or rifle fire. You were on top of them in no time. I met Japanese who had been fighting for fourteen years so they were masters at camouflaging themselves. We had slit trenches, cut long ways so we could lie down, but the Japanese had fox holes which were dug down so they were able to stand up to fire their guns. These were all linked together by passageways so they could move from one fox hole to the next. But they'd had a long time to prepare, we had to dig trenches as we advanced. You just kept going. Sometimes you never slept at all and although it was very hot in the daytime at night it could be very cold and you only had a ground sheet to wrap yourself in.

I can remember the first Japanese I killed. We came to this village where some fighting had taken place and there was an injured Japanese, apparently dead, on the ground. As we walked past I saw his leg move so I had to put the bayonet into him. It sounds a horrible thing to do but you just had to do it.

Another time we were advancing upon a village called Madaya, our platoon was leading and our section was a leading section, and I was the leading scout. And all of a sudden we came across these footprints which we recognised as Japanese, because they had very small studs in their boots which were close together. At first I thought they were American footprints but my friend Lofty said, 'No, that's Japs.' We didn't want to attack them because it was coming up to dusk. Any rate, we got to this village and settled down round the perimeter and all of a sudden all hell was let loose, the Japanese had got there before us. We had phosphorous bombs and burnt them out. We had no casualties, but they did.

If you came across a village and there were no civilians we knew that the Japanese were around. At another village we came across some civilians and all of a sudden they disappeared, then machine gun fire broke out. I can't say how many tons of shells we used

Resting in Burma

against them and in the end, when the bodies were brought out, we discovered that there had only been five Japanese fighting us and they had held up a whole brigade for half a day. One also has to bear in mind that when the Japanese were winning the war a lot of the Burmese and Indian regiments went over to the Japanese but when they could see a change of fortune they came back over to us.

We fought right through the monsoon and in the dried up river bottoms, because the ground was so hard, the water didn't soak away. We had to cross these rivers and many of us couldn't swim, some drowned. We had a bandoleer of bullets around the waist, and one on the shoulder, and our pouches contained grenades and phosphorous bombs. Sometimes we rode across on elephants but more often than not you just got across the best way you could.

Mules carried the large water containers and ammunition and food. I didn't see any mechanised vehicles until we reached Mandalay. We often were issued with bully beef, which was just liquid when you opened it because it was so hot, and what I called dog biscuits which were hard small round biscuits.

If you were ill, or injured, you were just left and you hoped that you would be picked up by the medics and passed down the lines. We were the fighter unit in front, and then there was the Battalion HQ, and the HQs of the four companies next, and then the Brigade came along behind and they had jeeps.

We always had a Chaplain with us. I'm not a religious person but I certainly was then, especially when you were going on a night patrol and knew what you were supposed to do if the Japs were there. Then I would say a prayer or two, and that would give me some comfort. The padre didn't carry any weapons, although he was up front with us, and he survived the journey all the way through Burma.

We had been in Mandalay for four or five days and it was reported that the Japanese were in Fort Dufrin. I was on patrol and was sure I could hear them and reported it to my Sergeant, who said, 'We'll soon find out if there is anything there or not.' There was Lance Corporal Sibley, another Private and myself. I was the leading scout and we got about fifty yards from our perimeter and the Japanese were there, they fired on us and we flew to the ground. We started to move, the Private was killed and I was shot right in the shoulder, the bullet passed straight through me.

Eventually I was loaded into a light aircraft and flown to a field hospital where I stayed for eight days. When I arrived there I was ashamed because I had to take all my clothes off for the first time in three months. My trousers almost stood up. In the jungle if you had a wash you just did your face and hands, unless you managed to get into a river, and then you had to be guarded.

I never felt any animosity towards the Japanese whatsoever. Although they were cruel, they didn't know any different. They were taught what they had to do and we were taught what we had to do. We saw some of the prisoners when we finally got into Fort Dufrin who were almost starving to death and were covered in sores, wearing only loin cloths. But what many people forget is that we, as a country, weren't all innocent.

Although the war ended in August 1945 we were still fighting in Burma and that continued until after I left at the end of 1947. I suppose we were doing then what the Army is doing in Iraq right now. It was called Duties Need to Civil Power. Both India and Burma got their independence in 1947. As far as I was concerned that period of time was worse than it was when we were fighting the Japanese because after the war officially ended you didn't know whom you were fighting. We had to contend with what we called dacoits, bandits, who were communists.

I had hoped to remain in the army and make it a career because I had climbed through the ranks from a Private, to Lance Corporal, Corporal, Lance Sergeant, Sergeant and finally Company Sergeant Major. Then we heard that our battalion was destined to stay for longer in Burma so I decided to go home. We were flown to Bombay where there was still a great deal of unrest. You still had to be very, very careful because they just wanted the British out. How could a few thousand British troops handle hundreds of millions of people? Four and a half weeks later we were back in England.

We landed in Southampton, went to Petersfield to be demobbed and chose some clothes - a suit, hat, shirts, underwear, socks and you could exchange your boots for shoes if you wanted, or your greatcoat for an overcoat, and I was back in Wincanton the same day. I thought Wincanton was beautiful, there was no mud, no jungle, no enemies hiding in the long grass and the electric lighting in the evening was wonderful. When I went away gas lamps had illuminated the town and now there was this wonderful bright electric lighting. Flags were strung outside the house to greet me and once again I could eat at the table wholesome beautifully cooked food and catch up with all that had happened to my parents and brothers and sisters in the intervening years.

The Probate Executive - Joan Whitmarsh

I was born in 1926 in Bourton, which is about 5 miles from Wincanton and lived there with my mother, father and sister who was nine years younger than me. I started school whilst living there and later attended Gillingham Grammar School. Whilst there I decided I wanted to be a secretary so I took Pitman shorthand lessons from Mrs Harris who also lived in Bourton.

We came to live in Wincanton in 1948 because my father worked for the building firm of Grant and Hutchings. He helped to build the cinema in Wincanton which is now the Community Church. I remember on the cinema opening night the family was given free admission. Father was also one of the builders working on the Rickhayes houses and because he was travelling every day from Bourton to Wincanton he was offered this house by the Council. We moved into it newly built but sadly father died in 1949 at only 55 years old. He had cycled backwards and forwards for years and years and only lived here for a few months. My mother died in 1984 at the age of 90, in this house, and here I am all these years later, still living in the same house; it having being modernised in 1986 when I acquired it from the Council.

After leaving school I went to work in Gillingham and then in 1947 I found a job with Rutter and Rutter, Solicitors in South Street which was founded in the 1800s and is still in practice today. I cycled all the way from Bourton to Wincanton and back, alongside my father. I was with Rutter and Rutter for 39 years, firstly as secretary to Mr Leslie Rutter, who was also the Coroner for South East Somerset at the time, and worked with the police, funeral directors, mortuary attendants and doctors so that the necessary hand written certification could be issued. Because Mr Rutter was the Coroner for the whole area we would have undertakers queuing up from Bruton, Shepton Mallet, Castle Cary, Yeovil - and all the villages for miles around. They were all anxious to collect the necessary certificates to enable them to proceed with the funeral arrangements.

I remember on one occasion there was a problem and a body had to be exhumed. They usually do this kind of thing as early as 2 o'clock in the morning and poor Mr Rutter had to be present. The Home Office pathologist came all the way from London to deal with the matter.

In later years I went on to manage the probate and trust department. Having dealt with many deaths they thought I had the necessary experience to study the area in depth and take over the department, which I did for some years. Very often I was so busy that I took work home to complete during the evening. I continued in this work right up until the time I retired.

I didn't really have a lot of time for going out in the evenings but occasionally I would go with my friends to the White Horse Hotel, which was a very fashionable place. They had a very good restaurant and when we lived in Bourton I would go there every day for lunch. At the back of the White Horse was a large room known as the Deanesly Hall, a very popular place, where dances were held every Saturday evening and at the Memorial Hall you could do Old Tyme dancing. Bands would come from surrounding villages - I remember one from Buckhorn Weston.

On the morning Mother died, at the age of ninety, she had cooked the lunch as usual. I had gone off to the office at half past eight, as I always did, and when I returned at one o'clock she was sitting quietly in the armchair over there. I greeted her, walked into the kitchen where the sauce pans were on the stove, went back into the sitting room and said, 'Mother, what's wrong?' she took a breath as if to say, 'Ah, you're here now,' and died. It was as if she had been waiting for me to come in so she could say goodbye. She had never been ill in her life.

I never expected to get married at all - I was a career girl really and had my mother to look after. I'd had one or two boyfriends but nothing serious. I had known John for many years, because we were both born in Bourton, and because my sister worked with his sister. He was a self-employed carpenter and joiner and lived with his parents until eventually they both died. He did a lot of work for a lady in Shepton Montague and I managed her affairs after her husband died and John would occasionally come into the office. When she was taken ill John came in with her instructions and we would chat away quite happily. After Christmas in 1984 he phoned me to say this lady had died and it was my job to sort out all her affairs. He had the keys to her house and went to collect the mail to bring it into the office for me to deal with. After that we became more friendly, and well……. we were married in April 1986 at the Parish Church, two years after my mother died, and had eighteen happy years together before John died in 2004.

The happy couple, April 1986

The Head is the Heaviest Part - George Masters

I was born in 1927 in Bradford on Avon, Wiltshire and then we went to live in Bournemouth where my father's mother lived. They had a boarding house where they could put people up for holidays and we lived in the basement. This was at the time of the depression and my father was out of work for a year. I think my mother took in washing to help the family budget. Eventually work was found in Wincanton and we moved into a house called St Joseph's in North Street three or four years before the war. I had two brothers and two sisters, but we lost the eldest sister to diphtheria when she was a child.

My father got a job as a car mechanic at Woodcock's which was opposite Clementina's and later on he went to work down at Wincanton Transport. The only vehicle my father drove was the local ambulance and I remember one day following on my bicycle all the way to Charlton Musgrove to collect someone who had come off his motorbike. In those days we had a beautiful general hospital in the town at Balsam Park, down the bottom of South Street which had been paid for by the people of Wincanton, and he was taken there.

My mother was a Cockney and she came down to the West Country to work as a cook in service in Bath, which is where she met my father. One story she often repeated was that when she went to work for some new people, as she was cleaning up, she found half a crown on the floor. It had clearly been put there to test her honesty. She didn't do anything about it at first and then she decided to pick it up and she slapped it on the table in front of the lady of the house and said, 'If you do that again, I'll leave.'

I played football and cricket at school and then when I left I joined Wincanton Town Football Club and eventually played on the team.

The grounds of the club were up West Hill, but it's all built on now. The apprentices from Wincanton Transport played football for Wincanton Town, making it difficult to get a place in the team. I cycled to the Cheriton and Horsington Football Club where I played for their team, along with three or four other Wincanton lads who were waiting for a vacancy in the town team. We didn't do any training, just got our boots on and played. During the war there were no fancy clothes to wear, you just turned up and played in anything. Our first set of jerseys were yellow and we wore black shorts and yellow and black socks.

We had just one football and that was made of leather which absorbed all the water on the field and became very heavy. If you tried to head one of those it would nearly knock your head off! We would pump it up but didn't have the strength to push the nozzle under the lacing because it was so firm. In fact there was only one player who had the strength to push the nozzle down and that was Henry Cook. When the Yanks came to the town we played with their footballs which were much easier to pump up. Of course their game of football was different to ours so we had to teach them how to play.

During the war there were German prisoners of war working on the farms and they were camped out at Charlton Horethorne. They would come over on their cycles, or walk, and we played against them. They weren't guarded at all. We didn't take a lot of notice of them really, we didn't know any different, but we were only young lads and didn't have much idea.

The Yanks were stationed all over the town but their camp was up West Hill. My father played cards with some of them at the Red Lion or the George Inn and he got pally with four of them, two of whom didn't want to go out with women, so he invited them back to our house for a sandwich or something to eat. They told us children to go round the back of their cook house and they would give us something to eat, as a way of saying thank you to my mother. The food they had was far superior to ours. We had hardly any-thing.......two ounces of sugar a week, a bit of butter, everything was all weighed out. But one thing we couldn't understand was that the Americans had all their food on one plate, the main course and their sweet. Very odd, we thought. For several years after the war these Americans wrote letters to us.

Handmade coffins - George on left aged 18 with brother Jack aged 14 in Mr Green's workshop.

I left school at fourteen. I had always wanted to be a carpenter and when my father went to see Mr Green he said I could go and work there. I started work there as a plumber's mate to Charmy Chilcott who charmed warts. He was a little man with a great big beard. Charmy lived down the common in a house that had been lived in by Italians during the First World War. You can still recognise the house because they must have had a sculptor there who put a plaque outside the front door. One day Mr Green came to see me and said that I was no longer needed as a plumber's mate. I was to go up to the carpenter's workshop, get a brush and start in one cor-ner and sweep up all the shavings. When he came to inspect it at the end of the day he said it was clean enough for a dance hall.

One of my first jobs was to help with the undertaking, making the coffins and collecting bodies. Normally I wouldn't have done this until I was sixteen but most of the men were away fighting. What I couldn't understand was the weight of the head - you had a real job to lift it up. My first client was a Miss Swan and here's a funny story, her grave is only three feet away from my parent's grave and they died fifty odd years later. Dealing with dead bodies didn't worry me one little bit and what amused my mother was that when I got home I couldn't stop washing my hands. I helped make the coffins for the people who were killed in the Templecome bombing....there were around eight or ten of them. Terrible.

One of the first jobs I had was working on the bank that had been bombed and I carried the tiles up to the roofers. The first lot I carried up three stories, a dozen of them balanced on my hip, and when I got to the top I didn't have the strength to hand them up to the mason. He told me to go back down and stack them on my shoulder so that he would be able to lift them off quite easily. I was up and down those three stories like a yo-yo all day long, that's all I did, supply the mason with tiles.

After five years apprenticeship I was a fully skilled joiner. The tools I used I inherited from my grandfather, and it's only a few

George taking a well earned rest

years since I got rid of them. My favourite job was putting on roofs. You had to cut all your timber to size, not like now when they come ready made. One day we had just finished putting the timbers up when the roof tilers arrived to do their job. They were cracking on quite nicely when suddenly a tile slipped and came flying down the roof, smashed onto a tiler's hands, and broke the bones in both of them. We were very upset, seeing this poor man so badly injured, so we went into our hut for a bit of a break. But our foreman made us go right back out and climb up onto the roof, otherwise we would never have done it and we would have lost our confidence.

The only disappointment I had in my life was not to be called up for National Service because I was doing my apprenticeship and it was considered foolish to break it. After five years the war in Europe had finished and they didn't want any more soldiers. Some of the men I worked with went to London to clear bomb damage and one of them was a fellow apprentice who had served four of the five years. This was considered breaking your apprenticeship so when he returned from London he was called up. Most unfair I thought. I would have loved to have gone but I couldn't break my apprenticeship. I would have been in dreadful trouble at home if I had!

Fine, for a First Timer - Ivan Parsons

I was born in 1928 in Chapel Alley, Wincanton which was adjacent to the Congregational Chapel in the middle of Mill Street. The chapel was still a chapel in those days but I don't remember any of my family attending. Our house was a very small cottage and I can remember being bathed in a tin bath in front of the fire. The lavatory was in a small lean-to at the back of the house.

When I was four years old I had a little tin car which you moved by pushing your feet along the ground, whilst sitting inside it, to get it to go. I would take it to the top of Mill Street, which is quite steep, take my feet off the ground and I'd run right down without stopping all the way to the George pub at the bottom. Just below where the Congregational Chapel is there is a large house and then another biggish house with a very low window. I came down the hill one day, turned sharp right, hit the wall and broke the window!

We moved from this cottage when I was five years old to Penn View, so called because you can see Penselwood. Then there were just 12 houses there and now there are around sixty. This was very modern and had an inside copper in the kitchen to heat the water. When I was about fifteen we moved to Rickhayes, which was a newish house, and it still had a copper in the kitchen. But wherever we have lived in Wincanton we have always had wonderful neighbours and friends.

My father was a ganger on the railway. He laid and repaired the railway tracks, the wooden sleepers and the metal rails, and during the depression he cycled from Wincanton to Evercreech every day to try and get work, a distance of nine miles in each direction. Maybe fifty men would be waiting around for a job and someone would come along and say, 'I need four gangers - you, you, you and you.' If he didn't get a job he would just cycle home again and try again the next day. This carried on for six months and it was the only time he was out of work all his life, but he did have many varied jobs.

He was also one of the three men who built the Cow and Gate chimney which dominated the town for many years. He wasn't the steeplejack, he was the labourer, the man who mixed all the cement and pulled it up in a bucket to the two steeplejacks who were working their way up the chimney. Later they had a petrol driven pulley to lift the cement. One day they told him to climb up. He didn't want to but he did. He said that after the first fifty feet, when he was shaking like a leaf, he became a bit more confident and when he got to the top he said it was fantastic.

Later on he was a mate on the lorries that drove from Cow and Gate all over the country. Two lorries would be hitched together, one acting as a trailer, and my father was the brake man. He travelled to places like Wales and Scotland delivering milk powder - their vehicle was called the Silver Queen. They would be away for days on end, almost a week. In fact my friend's wife's father, Cecil Curtiss, was the driver.

As a boy I always did my best not to misbehave too much when dad was away. When I became a bit naughty I hid out of mother's way under the kitchen table, which was in the corner of the room up against the copper. She would get hold of the broomstick and prod me with it - she knew how to quieten me down. I always knew what was coming and it wasn't very nice.

Mother worked at the skating rink as a packer for Cow and Gate. I don't know what she packed. It was a roller skating rink....anyway she was a packer and it was nothing to do with the rink because it was after the rink closed down.

I went to the local school down South Street where Doc Shapley was the headmaster. He wasn't really a doctor, it's just that once he played the part of a doctor in a play and so the name stuck with him. He was brilliant and had a wonderful personality. If he were teaching you history he would tell you about what it was like when he was a boy. If it were geography he'd tell you all about where he had been. He just made it very, very interesting. He gave us the cane regularly and when it broke he sent one of the seniors up the town to where the post office is now to buy two more. It's funny when you think about it, an ordinary shop selling school canes, but they did. One day a friend of mine, George Masters, went up the hill to buy two new ones and when he got them back to school Doc Shapley said, 'I'd better try them.' George held out his hand and the headmaster did try them! But he was a wonderful man and knew a lot about the world.

Mr Burt was the physical training instructor. We did a lot of gymnastics over the wooden horse and did balancing exercises on bars.

A physical exercise display with Mr Burt on the right.

In Church Fields, where the Council Offices are, we put on displays for all our friends and families to watch. Church Fields was a private house then and our display took place on the lawn. I was very happy at school, there was nothing I didn't like, and I became interested in everything I was taught.

When I left school at fourteen my father said, 'I've got a job for you.' 'No, you haven't, Dad,' I said, 'I'm going to work in the laboratories at Cow and Gate.' 'No, you're not. You are going to work for a living,' he said. He didn't consider working in a laboratory was work because he was a manual man. Anyway, he told me he'd got me a job as a mechanic. I was told to go down to Wincanton Transport and see Dick Lewis the foreman. When I got there I discovered that Dick Lewis was not the foreman of the mechanics, he was the foreman of the painters. Anyway, he said he would give me a job. For six months I didn't do anything but clean and scrape the vehicles and do all the dirty work. There were two other apprentices and they were given sign writing practice but I wasn't. There were days when I would go home and say to my dad, 'Oh, I don't like that job.' 'You'll stick it,' he said. And I had to stick it.

After six months I was given a sign writing brush and the number-plate of a lorry to copy, a square one as they were in those days. I practised this six times. I wasn't allowed to do it at work but had to take it home with me. The first attempt was thrown down the length of the paint shop with a cry of 'rubbish!' As it was made of metal it made a heck of a din. I tried again and again and all I got was, 'You'll never learn.' But the foreman never showed me what to do. On the sixth attempt he said, 'Fine.' I couldn't believe it. 'Fine. For what I call a first timer that is excellent.'

I had to learn every aspect of the trade, not just signwriting, but also cleaning, painting and finishing the full vehicle. First of all the vehicle had to be prepared by rubbing down. Then primer would be painted on, then it would be rubbed down again, then undercoating would be put on and you would rub that down again. Then you would put gloss on and rub it down, then gloss again, and then around two coats of varnish. I went right through my apprenticeship from 1942 to 1946 when I was called up for the services.

When I went for my medical I was hoping for a place in the RAF but in those days if you didn't have a relative who was already in that service, or had been in the past, they wouldn't accept you. So I was sent to the RAF Regiment, which was the army side of the RAF, and they did all the guarding of the aircraft on the bases. Within a week the Flight Sergeant came into the billet and said, 'I have eight lucky lads. You've all been transferred to the other side of the camp,' and we were in the RAF! I was an airframe fitter which meant I serviced the aircraft. I was based at Manston in Kent, near Dover. 'Hellfire Corner' they called it during the war because it was the first port of call for the enemy aircraft when they came across the channel. I had to service a lot of different aircraft including German Junkers freighters because it was a staging post. They would drop in and stay overnight to be serviced. There were Hurricanes, Tempests, Typhoons, Barracudas, Mosquitos, Avro Yorks, many different types of aircraft needing attention.

Although it was after the war there was still a German prisoner of war camp at Waterbeach in Cambridge and it was my job to look after one particular prisoner who worked for me. He made slippers out of old sack bags. His name was Adolph Stein Keirkner and we never saw eye to eye. He was very bitter that Germany had not won the war. We also had a German Naval Commander prisoner, he was no problem, and I used to play snooker with him.

I met the wife when I was down there in Kent and we eventually settled down here, back in Wincanton.

Awash with Tea - Peter Tucker

I was born in 1930 in Poona, India because my father was a Sergeant in the 9th Armoured Car Company. He had run away from home to join the army as a young man because he was put into a trade he didn't want, hairdressing! He was in the army before the First World War and during it he fought in the battle of Mons but he never would talk about it. He was wounded but went back again. He stayed in the army until 1931. My mother loved living in India but I was a very weak child and the climate never suited me, so when I was one year old we returned home to live in Wincanton.

My mother came from near Bristol and was in service at Hallatrow Court, near Bristol. After the end of the First World War my father was guarding German prisoners of war at Hallatrow and the two of them met. We became an 'army family' and each of my brothers and my sister was born in different army camps. When the Second World War started he volunteered for the army and served at Bovington and Tidworth. My sister went in the army and one of my brothers went in the army. I wasn't old enough but did my National Service after the war. I was looking forward to joining up and intended making a career there because I liked it so much but in the end circumstances did not permit this and I was needed at home.

In Wincanton during the war, where the tanker depot is now, was a tented camp where the Hampshire Regiment was stationed. Then they built the camp up at West Hill, where King Arthur's School is, and the tents came down. The Americans were good fun and would often drive us round the town in jeeps and would give you sweets and chewing gum. One Christmas they gave a party for children up at the Deanesly Hall, one Saturday it was for the evacuee children and the next Saturday it was for Wincanton children whose fathers were in the armed services. The food was wonderful, much better than our rations were.

The cinema operated right through the war and there were always queues to get in. I sat in the sixpenny seats right at the front. Behind them came the shilling seats and in the balcony they were two shillings or two shillings and sixpence. There were no refreshments sold, no ice creams, sweets or anything. Afterwards we had to walk home in the blackout. We rarely had torches because you couldn't get batteries for them and I never remember anyone being molested.

Where Anchor Hill garage is black Americans were stationed. They were segregated from the white soldiers and when the white Americans were allowed in the town the black Americans weren't and when they were allowed in the town the white Americans were locked in their camp. When you see the war films now and you see black Americans fighting along-side the white Americans you know it's just ridiculous because they were not allowed to mix. They would fight one another if they came across each other in the pubs. But the local people didn't mind what colour the Americans were. The black Americans were the labourers and leading up to D Day, all along Moor Lane, were heaps of ammunition shells stacked up behind the hedges with tarpaulin pulled over them. It was the black American's job to move them about. The shells weren't guarded, they were just left there until they were needed and then they were just moved on.

Peter on the left during Army training

When I was called up to the army my first camp was at Oswestry. I travelled there in my ordinary clothes where I was issued with my uniform. My own garments had to be wrapped up in a brown paper parcel and sent back home. I had never worn boots in my life and they were very hard and uncomfortable for the first few days. I enjoyed being in the army it was, after all, in our blood.

After doing National Service I returned home to live with my family in Balsam Park. I went back to work at the Council where I had first started working when I left school at 16. It was compulsory that your employers took you back for six months so I returned as a junior clerk. Eventually a job came up in the Treasurer's department as a rent collector so I took that.

First of all I had to learn to drive. The other fellows used to take me round in the van and I learnt to drive and collect rents at the same time. I collected money for the old Wincanton Rural District Council which comprised of thirty-two parishes. I was out every morning and afternoon collecting rent and three mornings a week I had someone to help me because I ended up collecting money from over two thousand council houses. At that time there was a massive council house building programme so the numbers I collected from increased as time went on.

My biggest problem was dogs. I was bitten twice. Mainly people would lock them up but occasionally they would roam loose and chase you. You had to work hard to steer clear of them.

There was an old lady over at Ansford who wasn't quite 'all there', just old age really, and she always reckoned there were German prisoners of war sowing dandelion seeds in her garden. As the rent increased she would never pay more than the amount she paid when she went to live in the house originally. Anyway she had some very kind neighbours who sorted her money out, making sure she paid the correct rent, and relatives would pay off the arrears when necessary.

Out at South Barrow was a house I was warned about. 'Whatever you do, don't accept a cup of tea in that house because if you do you will have to read a prayer.' They were very religious minded and if you accepted a cup of tea you were hauled into a little Church service.

The people I collected from became friends. If they were out you always knew where the key was to let yourself in to collect the rent. There was one house in Milborne Port where every fortnight, because it was a fortnightly collection, there was a cup of tea and biscuits waiting for me. One day she said, 'I'm going back to work again but you let yourself in. The milk will be in the saucepan on the gas stove, the biscuits will be on the table, you help yourself.'

Only occasionally would people not pay the rent, they would hide when they saw us coming, but we got it eventually. At the end of the financial year we had a big purge to collect it all in so that when the auditors came to audit that year's books we made sure that the balance carried forward was not too big, but in between we didn't bother all that much. We made sure it didn't reach a fantastic amount but it wasn't a great big problem.

All the money we collected we carried in our pockets. There were no special security arrangements like you would have to have now. It was a fixed round and you went to the same houses at the same time every fortnight. It would have been so easy for someone to have waylaid us if they wanted to but things like that just didn't happen.

When there were two of us out the one who wasn't driving added up all the money. We would then cash it up and if the amount of money collected didn't tally with the amount in the book we would have to make up the difference out of our own pockets. Anything over was ours. I think the biggest amount I lost was ten shillings, which was a lot of money then.

We had a rule amongst ourselves that we would never refuse a drink. In Henstridge there was a row of eighteen houses and in the first five I would have three cups of tea. People trusted us so much. So many people were working so we would let ourselves in, collect the rent, sign the book, lock up, put the keys back in their original hiding place and set off to the next house.

Up at North Brewham......well, the post office was at South Brewham and there was an old chap who lived in a council house at North Brewham and my instructions were, 'Be at South Brewham at 12 o'clock because Mr Beesely from North Brewham will be down at the post office to collect his pension and you have to take him back.' We did just that and he always had a cup of coffee ready for making. They were a nice old couple and when it was their 60th wedding anniversary they gave me a piece of cake.

Over time you became very much involved with the different families. You knew when people died, when they were born and when they got married. When we were married I received goodness knows how many wedding presents from the tenants. We were sort of friends of the family.

A Recipe For Slops - Ted Green.

I was born in 1930 in Templecombe in the Merthyr Guest nursing home. I was the eldest in the family, then there was my sister, Margaret, mother and father and we lived at 69 High Street opposite where I live now. One day, when I was about five years old, I came back from school and walked into number 69 and found one of the men who worked for us doing some painting. 'Oh,' he said, 'You don't live here any more. You've moved.' We had moved up to 73 High Street and nobody had bothered to tell me. It was at this house where my brother John was born.

My grandparents, who had lived in number 73, had moved across the road to the house which had been built by my great grandfather for his family. At that time I had two maiden aunts living in one of the houses opposite, my grandparents next door to them, and the house next door was owned by another maiden aunt. She was in an institution in Salisbury because her father wouldn't let her marry the person she wanted to marry and she had become a hymn

No. 73 High Street. Mother and guests

singing evangelist. I still have some of the old cheques that were paid for her keep. My grandfather, all the maiden aunts, my Aunt Harriet and cousin Cissie all died in the flu epidemic in the 1940s. I have a copy of the letter my father sent to his brother in New Zealand telling him of these deaths.

My father joined the Navy as a boy of 11 years old and was sent to Dartmouth where he became an engine room artificer. During the First World War he was at Jutland, and he was torpedoed twice in the Mediterranean. His elder brother, who should have inherited the family business, dropped dead playing football, Uncle Percy had emigrated to Canada, Uncle Frank had emigrated to New Zealand so dad was bought out of the Navy by my grandfather in 1926 to help run the business. I always think he would have been much happier staying in the Navy.

My maternal grandfather was born in India where his father had been a Troop Sergeant Major with the 5th Irish Lancers. He was Clerk to the Board of Guardians of Wincanton, who ran the workhouse, and the Clerk to the Rural District Council. Unfortunately my grandfather died young and it is said that the responsibility of the job weakened him. He often had to set off on the old Somerset and Dorset railway to retrieve girls who had bolted off from the workhouse. His responsibilities were a bit much and he died from a duodenal ulcer, leaving his wife with three daughters to bring up.

My father was the third generation of builders and undertakers established in Wincanton in 1835. My great, great grandfather was born in 1798 and he was described as a gardener but he apparently owned the land at the top of the High Street and the family has lived at this end of the town since that time. The pub Uncle Tom's Cabin down the road.....Uncle Tom was my great uncle and he built the pub for the labourers on the railway and at the back there was a beer garden for their pleasure.

Another ancestor had a cottage built on Flingers Lane, which was one time called Primrose Lane, and the family owned all the gardens behind the High Street. My great uncle had a nursery which came down the back of Uncle Tom's. My grandfather had an interest in Flinger's Lane and decided to build some houses up there on the nursery land. This upset his brother very much because it was cutting off the footpath to the beer garden. When grandfather was building he was not allowed to put up the scaffolding on his brother's land, which caused the family to fall out. It was many years later before they got back together. One of our workmen said his grandfather could remember at night throwing cabbages, which had fallen into the earthworks during the day, back over the wall because his employer's brother didn't want to be accused of stealing any vegetables.

I went to Gillingham Grammar School. In good weather I cycled there and one day in the early 40s I got as far as Clapham Farm when I saw there was something strange sticking out of the hedge. It turned out to be a short nose Blenheim bomber which had crash landed. The crew were sitting on her wing having their morning cup of tea! I stopped and had a chat and went on my way to school. When I came back the plane was gone.

Many teachers at school had left to serve in the forces during the war so there wasn't much career guidance going on. I left when I was fifteen years old to work in the Westminster Bank in Glastonbury, between two pubs - a lovely spot to be! Getting to Glastonbury was a lot of fun, especially for the immature person I was. The first time I went there my father took me and introduced me to my landlady, Agnes Harriman, whom I lived with during the week. Every Monday morning dad drove me to Cole where I boarded a train to Shepton Mallet. There I climbed into a taxi which took me to Wells. At Wells I got the bus to Glastonbury. The whole journey took 2 hours. In those days we had to work on

Saturday mornings so I didn't catch the train at Glastonbury station until 2 o'clock in the afternoon and I got home at 5 o'clock. I spent many hours sitting in the waiting room at Evercreech Junction. One day I got on the Pines Express by mistake, which went down to Bournemouth, and we shot through Wincanton. For some reason the train stopped at Templecombe and another one going in the other direction stopped opposite. I stepped out of the one I was on into the other one, travelled back to Wincanton, and arrived at the same time as the train I should originally have caught pulled into the station.

I stayed at the bank until I was called up for the forces in 1947. I went for my medical in Bristol and was sent to the Navy where I became what they call a writer. I had just swapped one set of ledgers for another! We were based in what were known as the stonehouse frigates, which meant I never left England. One posting sent me to Yeovilton where I spent all my time trying not to come home. After discharge I was called to the bank's head office in London where I was told by the principal that they were very pleased to be able to offer me a permanent job at the bank. Previously I had been temporary, and I had pleasure in telling him that I didn't want his job as I was going to work for the family firm.

Before the war I suppose you could say the family were well off. We had a tennis court and maids. During the war my father was involved in the Fire Brigade and went as far as Bristol fighting fires and my mother had a lot of responsibility running the business.

One night in 1939 I went to bed and woke up to find two strange children lying asleep on the floor beside me. The evacuees from Barking had arrived and four children didn't want to be split up because they were two brothers and two sisters. Mum said she would have them. My sister always said that mum wasn't keen on

Ted, first right, with two evacuees

girls so she shifted them off within a few months to other families but the boys stayed on. One of the evacuees complained that mum didn't know how to make 'slops' properly. We didn't know what they were but found out later - after the adults had finished their tea there would be a drop of cold tea full of leaves left in the bottom of the cup. Milk and sugar would be added to it for the children to drink. They were from a very poor family. We were in different worlds really, but somehow we got on together. One of the two brothers stayed in Wincanton for some time and became a delivery man. After returning to Barking he turned up one day with his young lady and told us he would never marry anyone my mother didn't approve of.

During this time the Yeomanry camped on the racecourse and kept their horses up there. It was a bitter winter and a lot of the horses died. The officer's horses were stabled at Angel Lane and the evacuees would go and clean the horse's saddles and the officer's leather belts for a penny a time.

When the men came back from Dunkirk we ended up somehow or other having officers billeted with us, and they were occasionally allowed to have their wives to stay with them. My mother was rushed off her feet looking after the elderly relations across the road, the officers living with us and helping out at the YWCA. I remember one of the wives washing her hair in the scullery - I saw her through the window. If my mother came across one of the soldiers looking lonely at some function or other she would send him to sit by our fireside and some of them came to stay with us when they were on leave. We also had airmen living with us. One lot were Polish who were only interested in killing Germans, so they were very dull people. Then we had some Canadians and they helped to dig the foundations for a bungalow that dad built out at Verrington. One of the officers had a guard with a gun outside his room, something to do with two Irish regiments getting mixed up and not being on speaking terms. One night the gun went off and the bullet went through the floor and landed on the dining room table where dad was working. I think it spoilt his concentration for a little while!

Medical Memories - Nora Elcomb

I was born in 1930 in the Merthyr Guest hospital, Templecombe. This was a general hospital given to the village by Merthyr Guest who lived at Inwood House in Henstridge. The maternity unit was upstairs and the general hospital wards were downstairs. We lived in Coombe Hill House, which is almost the last house as you go out of Templecombe towards Henstridge.

My father, Dr Edward Tustin, was the local doctor and he travelled up to a thousand miles a week covering his rounds which extended to the other side of Shaftsbury in one direction and to Evercreech in the other direction. He was initially the junior partner of the practice in Wincanton but the senior partner had a heart attack during the war, the middle doctor was killed by a flying bomb in London, so daddy was left on his own.

Just before D Day father joined the Army and was furious when he had to come back to run the practice. Mother employed endless locums and father would come back and sack them all and she would have to begin the process of finding replacements all over again.

Father did Caesarean sections at the local hospital, and mastectomies, gall bladder removals and all the little things. He was a general practitioner, not a surgeon, but in

*Dr. Edward Tustin -
from a charcoal drawing*

the early days you trained to do everything, and he did do every-thing in that little hospital which remained fully open as a general hospital until the Health Service came into being in 1948. Before this time all medical care had to be paid for. There was what was known as the Panel system. I think you had to get yourself regis-tered with a certain doctor and pay a small amount every time you wanted to see him for medical attention and then you paid for your drugs separately. In the country fees would often be paid by barter and father would be paid with things like eggs and birds, chickens and pheasants. A great deal of social work was done through GPs, sorting out family problems and quarrels. Sometimes he would be called out to a family for a medical reason but when he got there it wasn't that at all, there was just a crisis for him to resolve.

You would be surprised that as a member of a doctor's family I knew nothing about the patients, even though the surgery was part of the house. My mother knew the people but didn't know what was wrong with them. Confidentiality was something you just did, there was no great play about it like the fuss they make about everything nowadays. I am a doctor and did the odd locum surgery for my father. All his records were locked away and he had no receptionist or secretary. He had no nurse and if he needed a chap-erone he would take the patient to hospital. Because he was two miles from a chemist he was allowed to make up his own medi-cines. All the dangerous drugs like morphine were kept under lock and key. I can remember great Winchester quarts of cough medi-cine and I can remember one time asking how much his patients would take. He answered, 'It wouldn't really matter if they took it all!' The nastier it tasted the better it worked.

Before the end of the war we moved into Wincanton and lived on Bayford Hill. Initially the surgery was in what had been the ser-vant's quarters, and later on he moved his practice into town near the Methodist Church. Father was a great sportsman and would spend most Saturdays in the season walking around Wincanton with his gun and his dog seeing what he could shoot for the pot. He was also a very keen beekeeper. Unfortunately when he was 64, just before he was due to retire, he had a stroke and fell into the beehive and was stung by hundreds of bees. Fortunately he knew nothing about it and died without being aware of the pain.

I went away to Rodean School in Brighton when I was nine years old. Afterwards I studied medicine at Middlesex Hospital, which is where my father had trained, and three days after I passed my final exams I got married to a soldier and I practised my medicine wherever I could. Hospitals in those days had thirty beds to a ward, with a hand basin in the middle which was used rather more than it is now. There was none of this silly nonsense about no beds. If patients had to come in and all the beds were full extra ones would be placed down the centre of the ward. You packed them in wherever you could.

I had what you could describe as a fractured medical career. My husband's first posting was in Camberley and we had one half day a week and one weekend a month together. Next came Nottinghamshire and I got a job at Derby Royal Infirmary where my father had worked and where my grandmother had been a nurse. She always used to say, 'I was a nurse, my dear, when you paid to be a nurse.' Victorian ladies did not do that kind of thing and the family thought she was rather odd but when they became ill they couldn't wait to make use of her assistance. The family was quite wealthy but she married a parson so she was brought down to earth a bit.

My grandmother was as deaf as a post, something which had afflicted her when she was only in her forties. She was a very Victorian old lady always wearing long black skirts and a modesty vest across her cleavage. Her hair was beautifully done, piled up on top of her head, right up to the day she died at the age of ninety. When she became older she lived six months up in Staffordshire with her eldest son, who was a doctor, and then six months down here with my mother. That was the way you looked after people then. On the whole you didn't shovel them off somewhere, in fact I don't remember there being any old folk's homes.

Eventually my husband was sent to Cyprus, during the emergency, and I took a job in Hastings, but I was able to join him there some time later where I did locum work for a GP friend. After about eighteen months we were posted back to England to Wakefield in Yorkshire and I worked at Pontefract Infirmary as the casualty officer. Next came Kenya where I worked in gynaecological and infant welfare clinics with the Indian community. People lived fairly frugally but we didn't see the starvation that you see these days. Malaya followed. It took me ten months to work out there, this time for the army, because the army would not pay me the same rate as they would have paid a male doctor. They had never had a woman doctor before, the only women to work there had been clerks and schoolteachers, so in the end I wrote to the BMA and they supported my case.

When we returned to England I took up what was to become my 'specialism', which was family planning. The pill had just come in when we were in Kenya and you had to have different qualifications to the ones I had to dish it out, so I studied for them. To start with I wasn't supposed to prescribe it for anyone who wasn't married and of course, at that time, the age problem didn't come into it - it wasn't even considered. But the Family Planning Association was much more broad minded and I found I could do more or less what I felt was right. I think the introduction of the pill was an excellent move because I think it is a woman's right to choose whether and when she has her babies.

Our next posting was America where my husband was liaison officer. His job was to make sure that things like our bullets could be used in different country's guns. We were based in Washington DC for two years but I found it very tiresome because I couldn't work there without taking all their exams and learning the different names of drugs.

In 1965 we bought this house in Stoney Stoke and in the mid seventies we were finally able to make it our home. I joined Bath health district and returned to family planning and had a clinic in Radstock and others in Warminster and Frome. In 1990 I finally retired to spend more time with my horses.

Still Remembered - Michael Watts

I was born in 1933 at Sunnyhill Farm, Riding Gate which is at the other side of Bayford. I was the eldest of five children, three boys and two girls.

My grandfather had been a volunteer in the North Somerset Yeomanry and fought in the Boer War. The soldiers were expected to take their own horses but his dropped dead the day before he went. When I recently looked at his Boer War medal I discovered that his last two army numbers were the same as my last two army numbers! What a coincidence.

My father and mother came from Wells, father from a farming family, and I think it was my grandfather who found them the Sunnyhill Farm to rent. Originally he kept pigs and cattle but eventually he sold all his pigs to buy a petrol driven elevator which would carry all the loose hay to the top of hay ricks, when they made loose hay ricks. I can remember my father saying that casual labour at haymaking time was difficult to find because all the hay had to be forked up by hand. Once the elevator was on the farm we had all the casual labour we needed because the hard work had been taken out of the operation. The hay was delivered from the fields by a horse and sweep, the sweep being a large wooden like tray with prongs on it to sweep up the hay. We always had heavy carthorses stabled at the farm.

In 1938 my sister Pam was very ill and the doctor didn't know what it was. Coming to the conclusion that it was meningitis they decided to operate on her on the farmhouse kitchen table. Gallons of hot water had to be boiled on the open fire - there were no mod cons then. It was in the evening when the operation took place and the only light came from candles and tilly lamps. The doctors were Dr Tustin and Dr Coulson, from Wincanton, and the operation was successful.

In 1943 we moved to Snag Farm in Stoke Trister because it was a bigger farm. We took over all the stock and farm machinery. Before leaving Sunnyhill Farm my father had a farm sale and sold everything but an elevator and an unbroken cart horse.

On Sunday 25 June 1944 my sister Pam, my brother John and I were playing in a field just behind the farmhouse. We had a den, which was an old poultry house, and were playing along quite happily. John and I were inside the hut and Pam was outside. All of a sudden she shouted out, 'Look out.' Flying directly overhead, almost skimming the trees was a large American plane. There was an almighty crash and all we could see was a ball of smoke and flames.

We were frightened and ran away from it. We got to the top of the hill and looked back and we could just see the farmhouse through the smoke and flames. We ran down through the orchard, into the farmhouse through the back door of the scullery. As we went through that door an American serviceman came in at the same time. Mother was standing in the front doorway of the scullery and the American said to her, 'Is everybody all right?' Mother turned round and saw us three standing there and said, 'They are now.' Father was outside frantically trying to find us. 'They are now.' I will always remember those three words.

The plane was a B17G Flying Fortress named Old Faithful and was on its 37th flight. It was a large heavy plane and it had nose dived into the farmyard only twenty yards from the house. My youngest brother and sister, mother and father were inside the house and had it been half an hour later all the cows would have been in that yard waiting to go into the milking parlour. But even on such a terrible day the cows had to be milked, and the milking parlour was impossible to use, so the animals were led round the back of the blazing plane into another barn where they were milked by hand. I think it was about ten o'clock at night before all the jobs were finished. This meant that at only eleven years old I had to milk two or three cows by hand every day before I went to school and do the same job when I returned in the afternoon.

The plane had been on a bombing raid in France and its No 3 engine had been hit by enemy fire. It was limping back, got out of control and there was nothing they could do about it. There is a story that the crew deliberately flew round the town so they wouldn't crash on it - but I'm not sure about that. I think they were basically out of control. There were nine airmen on board the plane and all were killed and I can remember seeing them carrying the bodies out. Nowadays we switch on our televisions and see bodies being carried from war zones, but in those days children never saw such things and the horror of it is imprinted on my mind. Most of these planes had a crew of ten but for some reason this one only had a crew of nine. We had one fire engine come up, that was all there was in the town at the time, and then it seemed like the whole of Wincanton turned up to view the wreckage. It's amazing how many people in Wincanton will tell you they were first on the scene!

Michael Watts at the Madingley American War Cemetary by the grave of Pilot Lieutenant Peter Mikonis

When the aircraft crashed a piece of propeller went ricocheting across the farm yard, chipped a wooden door post, went through the door, went through another door and ended up inside a smaller building under a pile of animal bedding. A pig, which was being fattened for Christmas, was running round and round and we were a bit puzzled why and we couldn't work out what had caused the damage to the door. Some time later, when we cleared out all the muck, we discovered this lump of propeller under the bedding. This outbuilding was frighteningly close to the farmhouse and we could never get mum and dad to talk about the day the plane came down. What might have happened is too terrible to think about. My brother and sister, being younger than me, didn't fully understand so I never had anyone I could really talk to. Even now, all these years on, the emotion of it grips me so strongly I can hardly speak.

After the hard winter of 1962-63 we noticed something on the farm shining in a bank. I picked it up and it was the identification tag of the pilot, Lieutenant Peter Mikonis. We sent it to the American Embassy who promised to forward it to the family. When we had the 50th anniversary service the sister of the pilot was contacted and she came over with her husband, daughter and grandson. But she had no knowledge of what had happened to the identification tag. In 2004, when we had the 60th anniversary, this same lady made the journey again with her two sons and her daughter.

The Queue Went in Both Directions -
Betty Humphries

I was born in 1933, in either Poplar or Stepney in London; I'm not sure which. When I was two years old my mother, father, grand-mother, two brothers and I moved to Milborne St Andrew in Dorset where my parents ran the sub post office for thirteen years.

The white building, centre, became O'Keeffe's in the 1940's. This photo of the Market place was taken in 1900

We intended moving into Wincanton in 1945, but because a bomb had dropped on the Westminster Bank the shop and house we should have occupied was not fit to live in. It was in the High Street, 16 Market Place, just around the corner from the bank, and was in a terrible state so we didn't move into the town until 1947. The living accommodation was quite cramped. I slept in a little box room, my parents had another bedroom which they shared with my sister for a long time, my grandmother was in the back bedroom, and my two brothers slept in a tiny room over the stockroom when they returned from boarding school.

I went to boarding school in Wimborne when I was about eight years old and hated it. I loved my home and my parents and missed them so much. Occasionally my mother sent me a parcel containing chocolate creams, which I thought were horrible, and other things. Before I had even opened my parcel I would call out, 'Who wants my chocolate creams?' I never said anything to my mum because I really thought it was the only chocolate they could get.

I left school a few days before my fourteenth birthday and was very much looking forward to working in the shop the following morning. I was taken by a friend to Broadstone station and put on a train to Wincanton. The Reverend Mother at school had given me strict instructions; 'You do not speak to anybody.' I had never been to Wincanton by train before and when we arrived in Templecombe I had to change trains. I could have either gone to London or Bath and was terrified of getting on the wrong train. I summoned up all my courage and sheepishly asked a lady on which platform I had to wait for my train. In years to come I got to know this lady quite well and she often told new acquaintances of the time this 'shy, young lady came up to ask which train to catch.'

In the shop, as well as newspapers and magazines, we sold sweets, tobacco, wool and we had a little library at the far end of the shop because there wasn't a public library in the town. Across the road there was another newsagent called Smith's which also had a little library. Selling newspapers could be problematical. I was often made to get out of bed to deliver them for the delivery boys who didn't turn up. We had a boy who arrived for his round one day and got a bit wet, and his mother wouldn't let him do it again! I hate newspapers to this day, the very feel and smell of them....ugh!

In 1947 we were still on food rations and, of course, the rationing applied to the sweets we sold. Customers would come along with their ration books and we had to cut out the tokens with a special pair of scissors and then take them to the Food Office, which was next door to Clementina's. If we didn't take them to the office there by a certain time you would loose your supply of sweets.

Every Wednesday at the bottom of the town, just round the corner from the Primary School and before the Church, was a large farmer's market and this was the day we received our supply of sweets for adults. After our customers had been to the market they walked up Church Street to our shop to collect their sweet rations. Long queues formed in both directions right round the corner as people patiently waited for their turn.

On Saturdays the sweets were delivered for the children, and it was their turn to queue. All their sweets were stored in big glass bottles. Liquorice torpedoes, liquorice allsorts, jelly babies, bull's eyes and aniseed balls were very popular. We also sold imps which were like small cough sweets, and round hard chewy sweets called monkey nuts - they loved those. In those days gob stoppers were proper great big gob stoppers, not those silly little things they make now.

One day a very distinguished looking gentleman came in the shop. He said to my father, 'I don't suppose you have any Terry's Old Gold, have you?' My father said, 'No. I'd give my right hand to get extra supplies of those.' Some time later the Terry's traveller came and he said, 'What have you been up to, Mr O'Keeffe?' 'Nothing,' my father replied. ' Well, I've been told to increase your supply,' said the traveller. Dad was very puzzled about this because he hadn't done anything to make that happen. He was then asked, 'Did you have a very tall and distinguished looking gentleman come in the shop?' Dad said, 'Yes, I did.' 'That was Mr Joseph Terry and he was so impressed with you that he has increased your supply of chocolate.'

When we were married some of our customers were very generous and gave us wedding presents and I still have some of them all these years later. In that cupboard are two dishes given to us by a lady down Mill Street. Another lady gave us a sauceboat, which I still have, and then we received cake knives and all manner of things and were very grateful. All in all we had an interest in the shop for over fifty years.

Paraffin, Meths and Turps - Pamela Cave

I was born in 1937 at the Merthyr Guest Hospital in Templecome and was the only child of Nora and Basil Clementina. We lived in a house which my parents had had built at the top of the High Street. I went to a little private school, Lambrook House, situated at the bottom of Church Street and run by a Miss Fowler. When I was eleven years old I moved to The Hall School, Bratton Seymour, a boarding school for girls which also took in day girls from the surrounding area. When I left school I worked in the family business because I had always enjoyed helping during the school holidays, and as my father never enjoyed good health he was pleased I had taken an interest.

My grandfather, Thomas Clementina, was Italian, hence the name of the shop Clementina. He died several years before I was born at well over ninety years old. My grandmother was his second wife, his first wife having died. They lived in North Street, where my father was born, and also living with them was a daughter by his first marriage whom I called Aunt Pollie. Aunt Pollie and grandma kept a china shop and grandfather traded using a horse and cart. This was utilised to take the family to Mass on Sundays at Bonham Chapel near Stourton because there was no Catholic Church in Wincanton at that time. In later years Mass was held in my grandparents house in North Street. In the late 1800s grandfather gave £500 towards buying the land for the building of the Catholic Church. The house on the site of the Church, Acorn House, was demolished but the stables became St Luke's Hall.

When I was young two Sisters of Nazareth came to stay with us each year and father drove them to the large country houses collecting donations for the childrens' home they ran in Bristol. I went along for the ride and when I was old enough to drive I took my father's place at the wheel.

Children outside what is now Clementina's - before the shop windows were installed in 1936

My grandfather on my mother's side kept a cycle shop, Tucker's. At first they traded at the bottom of North Street and then in the early 1930s they moved to Pine House in the High Street. I can remember their workshop and as well as repairing cycles they repaired radios and travelled round the villages with a van exchanging charged accumulator radio batteries for flat ones.

In 1929 father took over Frank Buck's business, selling dairy utensils and items for the home, which was situated on the corner of South Street and Market Place, next to Albion House. In 1936 the premises in the High Street were purchased. It was a large townhouse and had been the first bank in the town, Stuckey's Bank, and at one time had been a solicitors. The Bank's large walk-in safes are still in the property till this day. Father had the present shop front put in, which for those days was very modern, and the show room at the side was built in the 1950s.

At that time many of our customers were farmers so we sold things like hay rakes, forks, pig troughs, barbed wire, galvanised buckets and bungalow baths in three lengths which were used for bathing in front of the fire. There were no plastics in those days and cooking pots and pans, plates, bread-bins, buckets and bowls were mostly made of enamel and frying pans were made of tin. I can remember the first time the Addis plastics representative called - most of his products were red.

The surrounding villages had no electricity so we sold two and three burner Valour paraffin cookers with an oven which could be placed over one of the burners. Paraffin was also used for lighting and we delivered 5 or 10 gallon drums in my father's estate car. This fuel was stored in 45 gallon drums in an open fronted shed and, whatever the weather, we would have to go outside to fill customer's own containers. Methylated spirits was also stored in 45 gallon drums and turpentine was in 10 gallon drums in the same shed.

We also sold glass butter churns in three sizes with two wooden paddles inside which were turned by a handle on the top. This churned the milk into butter which was later shaped by butter pats, which we also sold.

During the war there was not much available to display in the shop windows. One Christmas father displayed three dolls houses he had made, each of a different design, and lit by torch bulbs attached to a battery.

In my young days the flat above the shop was rented to the postmaster, Mr Taylor, and the crown post office was at 20 High Street. Since my marriage to David Cave in 1965 we have lived on the shop premises. In 1985 we sold part of our land at the rear of the shop for a housing development, known as Cash's Park, something which my father had planned as long ago as the 1960s. At the same time we donated around 2 acres of land, now known as Coneygore Green, to be kept as an open space for the enjoyment of the people of Wincanton.

By Royal Invitation - David Perrett

I was born in 1938 at 22 Penn View at the top of the town. My father had been born in Cucklington and worked at one of the big houses as a garden boy, prior to going in the Army. When the war broke out he was one of the first to go from Wincanton. My mother was left with two small boys to care for but that didn't put her off taking in two evacuees from Barking near London. Where she put us all I really don't know because we only had two bedrooms. The evacuees stayed with us for a few years and we have always kept in touch with them. When dad was discharged from the army he returned to work in Wincanton at the Cow and Gate factory.

One of my grandfathers was a postman. He lived in Mill Street and had seven children who all survived. He retired from the post office just before the war broke out and went jobbing gardening and was a fire-watcher down at the factory during the war.

When I lived up at Penn View I would often walk along the public footpath with my friends to play games in the old burnt out Rectory at Charlton Musgrove. It was a very exciting place for us to be and we spent many happy hours hunting in all the cinders for bits of old lead which we would then sell on to the scrap man for a shilling or two. The Rectory was eventually rebuilt and named The Coach House.

Because Penn View was only a two bedroom house it was considered to be overcrowded, although there was only me and my brother and mum and dad, and in the 1950s we moved down to the new houses at Balsam Fields where I lived until 1965. From there it was very easy for my brother and me to walk to the picture house, the cinema, twice a week - every Monday and Thursday.

After leaving school I went to serve my apprenticeship with a very high class firm of decorators called Stagg Brothers. Unfortunately they didn't have a lot of respect for their workers. We had to work on Saturday mornings in those days and often when we went back to the office to collect our wages they hadn't bothered to do them. It wasn't the fact that they hadn't got the money, they just couldn't be bothered. I was single then so it didn't matter too much to me, I could always pick mine up on Monday mornings, but those who were married with families had to stand there and wait for their wages to be made up. We were never given anything for Christmas and if we had a quarter of an hour off it was taken out of our wages. At times I felt like leaving, particularly when I knew I could earn a pound a week more working down at the factory. One of my workmates told me that it was better to earn a pound a week less when doing your apprenticeship because you would get two pounds a week more than down at the factory when I had finished my five year apprenticeship. How right that was.

In those days paint had large amounts of lead in, which we now know is very poisonous. We were told to drink a lot, mostly milk, to get it through our systems. Food rationing was still in place and because we were classed as manual workers we were entitled to an extra allowance of various things, like tea and sugar and cheese. Mr Stagg had to go down to the food office, which was where Clementina's car park is now, to collect our extra allowance. He carried all the food back to the shop and told each of us how much we had to pay.

About eight years afterwards I had a very bad car accident and ended up in the Royal United Hospital in Bath. The police took my parents all the way from Wincanton to Bath that night because they didn't think I was going to survive. The accident happened on a Tuesday night and the chap who was driving the car went back to work the following Monday but because I had caught the full impact I was off work for a year. At the time I was a member of the

Young Conservatives and they rallied round to help very well. In all the four months I was in hospital there was never a visiting time when somebody didn't turn up. What made me feel very important was that on a couple of occasions our MP, Commander Maydon, came to see me outside visiting hours.

Shortly after I came out of hospital I went on holiday with the Young Conservatives. We had fixed up to go to the South of France and we went from here to London Victoria and then to Eastbourne where we caught the boat. We travelled down to St Raphael on the train and only three weeks before my leg had been encased in plaster. I was still on crutches and without the help of friends I couldn't have gone. We stayed in a sort of a holiday village on the sea front, the boys in one house and the girls in another. I can remember it was very hot and it was right on the beach. One day we travelled on the bus to Monte Carlo and we all clubbed together to have a couple of goes on the gaming tables, another day we went into Italy. There were some lovely sandy beaches there but a chap on two crutches and sandy beaches don't go together, so my friends carried me down into the sea so that I could swim.

David Perrett, Chairman of Wincanton Young Conservatives, with pop star Ruby Murray at the 1961 Wincanton Annual Walking Race.

My work took me into lots of the big houses like Yarlington House, Horsington House, North Cheriton Manor,

Cadbury Court and Redlynch House where the Countess of Suffolk lived. I worked at Cadbury Court both as a lad working for Mr Stagg and then later when I worked for myself. As a young man one of my jobs was to go down to the kitchen to get the tea twice a day. The cook, Nellie Kempster, would cut me off a great big chunk of fruitcake and I had to stay there to eat it so the others didn't know.

Whilst I was working at Shanks House, Cucklington I had an invitation to go to a garden party at Buckingham Palace. I was still in the Young Conservatives then and doing a bit of charitable work for the Cancer Campaign and Somerset Blind, so whether it was something to do with that I don't know. This was before I was married, in my twenties, so as a single man I couldn't take anybody with me to share the occasion. It was one of the most wonderful experiences I have ever had, it was unheard of for an ordinary working class boy to go to Buckingham Palace.

My customer who lived at Shanks House got to know of my invitation to the palace and she came to see me one day and said, 'I hear you have an invitation to the palace. I don't know how on earth someone like you can possibly get one. But you have one, and if you take my advice you will see quite a bit of the royal family. Everybody thinks they will come out of where you will be standing, just outside the Morning Room. But they wont.' She gave me directions of where to stand and wait.

When I arrived at Buckingham Palace I went through the Morning Room, through some French windows and down a flight of steps. I did exactly as she told me and there were only about half a dozen people waiting and there were crowds of people everywhere else. I stood there for a while and began to panic a bit, I didn't want to miss anything. Then a big Rolls Royce pulled up and out climbed the Queen Mother, and then at 4 o'clock the Queen, Prince Philip,

Princess Alexandra and several other members of the royal family came past me, as close as I am to you. I can't remember what the Queen looked like, there is so much to take in, but I can remember just how discoloured the Queen Mother's teeth were. A silly thing to remember, really.

There was a great long marquee and because it was a lovely day it was all open. The Queen and the other members of the royal family went down different gangways that had been made for them and occasionally stopped to talk to someone or other. Eventually they went into their own marquee to be with their invited guests. The rest of us enjoyed cucumber sandwiches and vol au vents, provided in those days by Joe Lyons.

In time I left Stagg's, worked in Sherborne at the ironmongers for a while and then returned to Stagg's until he made us all redundant because Mr Stagg wanted to retire. At the time my wife, who was expecting our first child, had just given up her work in the bank and there I was redundant. I thought my whole world had collapsed. But it was one of the best things that ever happened to me. Firstly I got a job delivering milk, starting at around 5 o'clock in the morning, and I had often finished my round by mid day. One or two people asked me if I would like to do a bit of decorating for them, Stagg's having given up had left a bit of a void.

After a while I realised that one job had to go so I gave up working as a milkman and set up in business as a decorator and in thirty years of working I was never short of a job. After about ten years by myself we heard on the grapevine that the old Stagg's shop was up for sale so we bought it. My wife ran the shop, selling paint and wallpaper, and I ran the decorating side with the help of a couple of chaps until I decided to retire at sixty through ill health.

Two Near Squeaks - Sam Bartlett

I was born during the war in 1940 in Queen Camel, not Wincanton, because my mother's eldest sister lived there. Also there had been lots of warnings about possible bombings of the Cow and Gate milk factory. The buildings down there were camouflaged with brown and green paint.

My father was the local butcher, as was his father. Two years after I was born my sister was born. Funnily enough both my mother and father, although they were not related, had the same surname. We lived at 2 High Street, right in the middle of town in the market place, where the delicatessen is now. The marble on the front of the shop is still there to this day. It is a very large three-story building with cellars where my father used to salt beef and tongues and I remember it was very damp. Up the side of the house is a road leading to the dance hall which is now used for discos. Behind the shop were garages where my dad kept his two delivery vans. He would visit the markets and choose which animals he wanted and then take them down to our own slaughter house which is still at the bottom of town.

My grandfather, around Christmas, would go to the Wincanton Market Christmas Fatstock Show and buy the champion beef. Hens, geese, ducks, and sides of beef would be displayed hanging outside the shop. There was great competition with Mr Loud, the butcher across the road! Grandfather was a very astute man and during the 1930's went around buying up everything he could lay his hands on. I have been a farmer all my life and he bought my farm out at Charlton Musgrove for £10 per acre. He also bought houses out at West Coker and East Coker and some land out at Anchor Hill which is now the by-pass. He had bits and pieces all over the place. My father was a cattle dealer and at farm sales he bought all manner of things like pictures, grandfather clocks and staddle stones.

When my father was a young man a rather snooty gentleman farmer from Cheriton would come to the market on a Wednesday in his pony and trap. After he had sold a few cows he would go up to the Dolphin pub and get really sozzled, so drunk he was incapable of holding the horse's reins, so the barman would load him into the pony and trap and the pony would find its own way home.

The road at the side of our house led to the Deanesly Hall and in the evenings during the war soldiers slept there. It was a bit like a transit camp for soldiers on the move from one place to another. In the summer my mother would put me outside in my pram to get a bit of sun and fresh air. One day she heard a sort of scraping noise and ran outside to discover that one of the army lorries was backing up the lane, pushing my pram along with its back wheels. That was my first near squeak!

The day the bomb dropped on Wincanton I was three and a half years old. The very first thing that I can remember is waking up and thinking, 'Who is throwing glass down the stairs?' This was 1944. I went out onto the landing and it was covered in glass from the shattered skylight up on the roof. The bomb had hit the Westminster Bank which was just round the corner from us, so at the back we were almost behind each other. The day before the bomb my mother had done her spring cleaning and had turned my bed round the other way. When the bomb landed a great big brick came through the window and crashed onto the bottom of the bed, which the day before was where my head had been. That was my second near squeak! Lots of damage was done to the house and we had a tarpaulin on the roof for about six months afterwards. Apparently the Germans were on a raid to Bristol and got intercepted. I understand that the plane had already been hit and so they jettisoned the bombs and turned round. Only one landed on Wincanton and the others fell in the fields round about.

My father, being a butcher and having a reserved occupation, was never called up to serve in the forces but was in the Home Guard. For the next three or four weeks after the bomb dropped all they did was clear up wills and legal documents which had been blown around the town, most of it had landed in the White Horse car park. There was no money around because for some reason the bomb didn't blow the safe open. The Home Guard used a shed down at our slaughterhouse to keep their armaments in, the guns and things like that.

One day there was a knock on the door and a man stood there and asked if there were any stray cats around. He wanted to catch them, kill them and sell them in London as rabbit meat. When cats are skinned they look just the same as rabbits so they wouldn't have been able to tell what they were going to eat. We only had a pet cat and guarded it carefully, but there were stray cats in the White Horse Hotel car park.

During the war the Mendip hills were used as a storage place for tanks waiting for the invasion, and all the way up those hills most of the lanes were closed. My father had a friend who lived there, he was a butcher cum cattle dealer, and had a permit to go on the Mendips. We saw hundreds of tanks lined up in the roads, covered up waiting for D-Day. A lot of them came through Wincanton to get to the South Coast and one day one of them lost control and went right through Buxton's jeweller's window.

Every Christmas we would have to wait till about 2 o'clock for our Christmas dinner because my father and one of the local doctors went up to the Town View workhouse to carve the turkeys and then went around serving the people who lived up there. It was a big house mostly for single old men and at the side was an annex for five or six down and out families to live in. The old boys would keep half a dozen pigs at the top of the garden and feed them with

Sam Bartlett, Centre front row, holding down his cassock to hide his wellington boots.

all the swill from the kitchens - it was their job. Every six months, when the pigs were fat, one of them would come to dad for slaughtering and the rest would go to market. I would go up with my father and pull these pigs down through the garden by their ears and their tails, they would be squealing away, and we loaded them into the van and took them off to market. The same day dad would buy another half a dozen young pigs and take them up to the workhouse so they could fatten them up.

I was a choirboy at the Parish Church for eight years. During the summer holidays every Monday I would go to Sturminster Newton market with my father. Unfortunately Monday was also choir practice night so it was a bit of a rush getting back in time for the

5.30pm start. One night they were going to have a photograph taken of the whole choir outside the Church. I was head boy, so it was important for me to be in the picture, and I didn't have time to go home and get changed and when I sat down my wellington boots stuck out of the bottom of my cassock. The photographer spotted this and insisted I pull the gown right down so that I was almost standing on it.

My father's slaughter house was down by the railway station which, on a Saturday during the summer months, was very busy with trains full of holiday makers going down to Bournemouth. The A303 used to go through the town and the railway bridge was only 13′ high. Everything on the main road had to either go under the bridge or do a detour. The trouble was that sometimes the drivers forgot about the bridge. I was down at the slaughterhouse many times on a Saturday helping my father when there would be a bloody great bang as another load of straw hit the bridge. We would often have two layers of straw dumped at the bottom of our track. One day there was one almighty smash when an army mobile crane with a jib over the front, came flying up the road and hit the bridge so hard that the whole bridge was moved. All the trains had to be stopped in each direction until the engineers came to move the rails back over and made it safe. But it was only out of action for two or three hours.

One day a circus was going to perform at Yeovil and they had this giraffe in a converted London double decker bus. They got down to the bridge but couldn't get through and so had to turn round to do a detour via Horsington and Cheriton. Going down towards Horwood they didn't negotiate one of the bends correctly and finished up in a ditch. For about three days afterwards the local farmer, Les Phillips at Suter's Farm, had this giraffe in his shed whilst they repaired the bus.

When I was a young man I didn't fancy being a butcher and so, after leaving Sexey's School in Bruton, I went to the farming college for Somerset, Cannington Farm Institute near Bridgwater. My grandfather had, in the 1930s, bought a 100 acre farm at Charlton Musgrove and the tenant there was getting old so at the age of 20 I became a partner and farmed Channel Island cows, Guernseys, for 37 years.

The milk was sold to the Cow and Gate factory at the bottom of the town and every day I would deliver it there in churns on the back of a pick-up truck. Because Channel Island milk had a higher butter fat content I received a bonus for it. For the first 30 years this milk was kept separate from the other milk and taken to London to be sold in places like Harrods. There were two tankers especially for this milk and they were painted yellow instead of the silver ones which collected the other milk. In later years, when everybody was slimming, it wasn't so much in demand and so it was just mixed in with the ordinary milk.

For nine months of the year 80 per cent of all the milk at the factory was taken to London. There were around 100 tanker drivers based in the town and during the night every ten minutes a tanker would set off on its journey to one of the big cities. Also milk from Devon and Cornwall would be driven to the depot, the drivers would change, and off it went to wherever it was going to be delivered. Every farm for miles around kept cows and there was a fleet of 50 churn lorries going round locally collecting milk.

All the tankers had to go for a special inspection and be weighed. They were filled with water but one day someone had only half filled one of them. The driver drove round the bend, the water moved, and the tanker turned over, right outside the Millers Arms down by the Church.

I didn't live out on the farm but continued to live with my parents in Wincanton. In the winter of 1962-1963, when the snow fell really heavily and I couldn't get back into the town, I slept on the floor of the house next door to the farm for three nights. For the first couple of days I had to throw the milk away because it was going off. Then we had to dig ourselves out and get the milk to the factory with tractors and trailers. You've never seen as many tractors and trailers, all lined up on the A303 patiently waiting to deliver their milk to Cow and Gate. When we got there it was chaos. There was hardly any electric and the tippers which tipped the milk into the machines wouldn't work.

The weather also led to problems with the milk tankers because they were snow bound. Some of the milk was put on the railway because a branch line went right into the factory so that rail tankers could be filled. There was such a stockpile of milk to be got out and after about two days they managed to clear the road out of Wincanton. What they did was get about 15 tankers lined up with a snow plough on the front one and they closed the one way system and went up South Street past the school to the A303, as it was then. They got to the other side of Mere and then got stuck there for two days. Some of the roads were so compacted with snow and ice that the only way they could be cleared was with pneumatic drills.

In the early 70s we stopped using milk churns, when the government decided to go for bulk tankers, so the churns had to be thrown out. We were given a grant so that we could have a bulk storage tank installed on the farm. I was one of the last farmers to have churns and Wincanton was the last factory in England to tip churns. Milk had to arrive at the factory at a certain temperature and cooling it in the old churns took a lot of time and water. When the milk went into the new tanks it was cooled automatically so it saved us a lot of work.

During April and June when there was plenty of milk, too much for liquid milk consumption, it was either sent to Chard for cheese or it was dried. A lovely smell drifted over the town as the steam came off in the drying process, and it was made into Cow and Gate baby food. It was an interesting process to watch. It came out of the dryers on rollers and in long hard sheets, like paper, and was then crushed into powder before being packed into tins.

After a few years they sold the Cow and Gate baby food to a Dutch company and decided to make cream rice pudding and become competitors to Ambrosia. They bought in a million pound machine from Germany, which tinned the pudding, but it never actually worked properly and within six months it was all scrapped. They spent millions on trying to keep this place going. A new weighbridge was installed in the mid 80's, costing a fortune, so they could bring in bulk tankers from the farms, weigh them and put the milk straight into the factory. The second lorry they had on the weighbridge when the bloke got out he had forgotten to put the brake on. The lorry rolled down through the Cow and Gate yard, across what was the A303, and smashed into the Fire Station at the other side of the road. After that they never used it again.

Eventually I sold the farm at Charlton Musgrove. I miss the cows but look back contentedly on the many happy years I spent farming.

Boating, Fishing and Milking - Brenda Jeanes Shave

Brenda and Binky the cat outside Mr Marsh's stables.

I was born in 1942 at 9, South Street, opposite Rutters solicitors but my ancestors, here in Wincanton and the surrounding villages, have been traced back to 1736. I was the first child to be born. My mother had a rare blood condition which meant that all the subsequent children she gave birth to died, two brothers and two sisters. Had it happened nowadays they would have just been given a blood transfusion but in those days they didn't have the expertise. Eventually Dr Everet told her she shouldn't have any more babies or she would lose her life.

Mum and Dad lodged with a man called Mr Marsh who was a blacksmith. As a small child the cart horses coming to be shod seemed huge to me. We had our own kitchen, bathroom and bedroom so we were completely separate. Mr Marsh was a nice old man who would stand outside at night studying the night sky and he could tell you just by looking what the weather would be like the next day. Every single night he cooked and ate a boiled onion to keep away colds, he never had one, and he lived to be ninety odd years old.

Dad, Mr Marsh and a man who lived opposite the Cow and Gate factory used to go fishing for eel, carp and chubb and they sometimes took me with them. We went out to Compton Pauncefoot to Lady Blackford's lake; we were allowed to go there because Mr Marsh shoed her horses, and I can remember the butler wheeling Lady Blackford, dressed all in black, around in a wheelchair. When we caught the eels we didn't throw them back in but wrapped them in newspaper and then bashed them on the head, hopefully to kill them, and took them home to cook. On one occasion, when they were put in the kitchen sink, they mustn't have been dead because they started to swim around.

My father collected milk from the farms and delivered it to the Cow and Gate factory. I went with him, sometimes in the cab and sometimes balanced on the top of milk churns on the flat bed of the lorry. It was fun. My favourite farm was out at Yenston on the big wide sweep of the corner. The farmer took the lid off one of the milkchurns standing there to be collected, tipped some milk into it, and all the farm cats came out to drink the milk. Once when I was there I counted thirty seven cats. It wasn't very hygenic - the lid was put straight back on the churn without being washed.

When I was fifteen I started work and saved up all my wages to pay for a boat kit which I bought from a factory over at Milborne Port. Dad and I built it between us and we tested its sea worthiness in the big deep concrete cooling tanks down at the Cow and Gate factory. Neither of us could swim, we didn't have any life jackets, but we dropped the boat into the water and stood in it and, yes, it did float! We painted it admiralty grey and took it onto the River Stour to launch from the farmyard of one of the farms dad visited, where the river ran right through the farmyard. We didn't know how to row so we just paddled the best we could, we couldn't see round any corners because it was so bendy, and we were still without life jackets!

We then became very adventurous and took the boat down to Hamworthy where my aunt and uncle lived, just across the road from the sea. They had a slipway from where we could launch and by this time I was the proud owner of a life jacket and an outboard motor. One day the water board decided to repair the weir. The water went down and down and the area from where we launched our vessel turned out to be so deep that you could stand two double decker buses, one on top of the other.

Because my father worked for the milk factory we were allowed free milk. It was one of my jobs to go down there to collect two pints of milk each day. This was measured out very carefully by Mr Elliot, who seemed very stern. Mr Goodchild was much more generous and would give you a can full.

My grandmother lived at Overton Terrace and grandad had a small-holding with goats, chickens and pigs up Flingers Lane. At the top of Flingers Lane was a field where there was a big crater made by a bomb falling during the war. This was one of our playgrounds where we played roly-poly. Our house was next to the bank that had been demolished by a German bomb and the remaining bit of ruin became another exciting playground. Granny took in washing from Mr Green, the undertaker, and she used flat irons which she heated by the fire. There were washing lines all over the downstairs room so the washing would dry in wet weather. We played with the animals in the smallholding and would look over the wall where there was Loads butchers, which is now the car park, and see all the animals ready for slaughtering. From the schoolyard we could peer over into the market and see all the animals waiting to be despatched - but this was the country and cattle ready for slaughter was an every day occurrence.

My other grandparents lived on a farm out at Charnage, the other side of Mere. My grandad was head herdsman and my gran was milkmaid, my oldest uncle looked to the horses and my other uncle was a shepherd. I loved going up there to play because I was allowed to milk a cow. I sat on a traditional three-legged milking stool and carried the milk back to the dairy in a wooden yolk which fitted across my shoulders with two buckets suspended from them. Riding on the carthorses, which were used for ploughing, was great fun but my legs were too small to fit over the girth of the horse so they just stuck out like broomsticks.

My grandmother wore a floral crossover pinny and her long hair was wound into three 'buns', one over each ear and another at the back of her head. The lavatory at the farm was outside in the garden and the contents were collected in a bucket and tipped into a great big hole at the bottom of the garden. There was no electricity and we had to use candles. When I stayed at my grans I can remember going up the spiral staircase, carefully carrying a candle to light my way to a feather bed. In the kitchen was a big, black range with a fire in the middle and ovens on either side. In front of the fire was a large fireguard and one day I was climbing on it and fell right between the fire and the fireguard!

My great grandmother did fall into a fire. She was a very old lady at the time and somehow toppled in. I remember my great grandparents clearly. They lived in a tiny cottage up at White Cross near Stourton and I can remember my great grandad taking me out for a walk one day up into the wood. Where there was a bit of a dip in the ground there was a great big snake. He threw a stone at it but I can't recall what happened to it. It must have been an adder or a grass snake. I was about five years old at the time.

Mr great aunt was a housekeeper and worked in a big house where King somebody-or-other went to stay and he gave her a clock which I inherited. Unfortunately we had burglars so that was the end of that. When she stopped working, this aunt lived in a little wooden bungalow with a few animals, until one day it burnt down and she lost all her possessions. That meant she had nowhere to live so for years she came to us for six months and went to another nephew in Bournemouth for six months. Her hands were dreadfully burnt, all the fingers drawn in to a tight ball, and her face was burnt and the poor woman looked so withered so, to me as a child, she looked like a witch. She always wore black and would walk up the town when it was two-way traffic and would just step off the pavement without looking, right in front of any vehicle. We often had irate drivers knocking on the door complaining that they had nearly knocked her down.

When I was fourteen years old I joined the Red Cross and all our meetings were held once a week in the conference room at the Cow and Gate factory. It was a very active branch, there were four women and fourteen men and we practised bandaging and artificial respiration. The men were allowed to be on duty at the racecourse but it wasn't deemed right for the ladies to go up there, it was considered too rough. They were real gentlemen in those days! I was the Assistant Cadet officer teaching young children first aid.

One day as I was walking down the street. Out of the corner of my eye I was aware of a motorbike coming towards me. All of a sudden it wasn't there and I thought, 'Where did that motorbike go?' I shot up the road and found the rider had fallen off his bike after hitting a dog and he was on the road behind a car. The dog was fine and had run away. He said, 'It's OK. I'm all right,' and off he went. A few weeks later we had a very hard snowfall and early in the morning I heard the screeching of brakes and a loud bang. I flew out of the house and lo and behold it was the very same motorcyclist laid there in the road! I can't say who was the most surprised - him or me. To this day I don't know who he was but he had fallen off his bike and had slid on the compacted snow all the way down the road.

A Musical Family - Yvonne Rogers

I was born in 1942 at 1 Rickhayes, where we lived with my grandparents for a short while, and when I was very little I shared a bedroom with both of them. My grandfather was a postman in Wincanton and on Christmas morning he had to get up early to deliver the post. One Christmas Day, very early, he said I could get up and open my presents. My father was awakened by the noise I was making and came rushing into the room to see what was going on. He was very cross with grandad.

My father was a rating officer in the council offices in Wincanton and later in Yeovil. My mother's final job was secretary at the Primary School. She went along there as a relief worker because somebody was off sick and stayed for 35 years until she retired.

My family has had connections with the Wincanton Silver Band for generations. My father's mother was a Chatfield and four of her brothers played in the band. We still have some members of the band playing who were instructed by Uncle Ray Chatfield and some of them, now married, were Chatfields. My grandfather played the bass, my father the baritone and when I became nine years old I started to play the tenor horn and my brother, when he became nine, learned to play the euphonium. My daughter-in-law's instruments are the cornet and horn and she runs a learners' group every week and also plays in the band, as does my son who plays the bass. Our three grandchildren are also keen members and play horn, cornet and cornet. Then there are two cousins - it's a real family meeting!

But ours is not the only family involved in the band. There are also the Parsons, the Shaves, and the Coombes. The Musical Director's son plays E flat bass.

Wincanton Town Band 1987. Yvonne Rogers, 2nd row from top and 3rd left.

When I started to learn to play the cornet, followed by the tenor horn, I didn't join the band immediately because the town band didn't have a learner's section. I started with the Wessex Youth Band but it was only a small group which eventually fizzled out so the town band had to start a learner's group. When I was a child you stayed in the town and stayed in the band, so it was easy to go along to band practise, but now they have to travel further afield so you usually lose these youngsters after a while.

Most bands in this area are struggling to find enough players and if you want to enter competitions you need a full band. Competitions are taken much more seriously nowadays and there are many more of them to enter. We are rehearsing now for a competition and in the week running up to the contest we meet three nights that week. In 1998 and 1999 at the West of England Championships we qualified for the National Championship, a great achievement.

Musical instruments are very expensive to buy. Quite a few years ago we were fortunate to receive a Lottery grant....they probably need replacing again by now. But when the band was formed in 1890 a group of trustees purchased a set of instruments which were then loaned to the players. You have never had to buy your own instrument, you've always had one provided.

Uniforms can also be a costly problem but we had two legacies which enabled us to buy some new ones. We have worn bottle green with gold trimmings for years now. When I was younger not much gold braid was used, because it was very expensive, so the uniforms were much plainer.

The band has travelled to our twin towns in both France and Germany and we are always well received. Once we stayed with a family in France and our son was put in the same accommodation, much to his disappointment - at his age he didn't want to be stuck with his mum and dad. Anyway our hosts turned out to own a restaurant and bar and very generously said we could help ourselves to whatever drinks we wanted. I think our son changed his mind after that.

The rehearsal rooms were at one time in St Luke's Hall and then moved to the Congregational Church in Mill Street, and then to the parcel hut in the railway station. After that they moved up to King Arthur's School and finally we have ended up in a couple of Mr Hopkins' rooms over by his office.

We play both at Wincanton Armistice Sunday and Shepton Mallet Armistice Sunday. I think that the war memorial in Shepton Mallet must be the coldest place in the world to play a musical instrument. Last summer we played at Stourhead, Chideock and Charmouth and we also hold concerts in the Wincanton Memorial Hall . When we can we play at the Carnival but Wincanton is a hard place to march and play, the hill can be a bit of a challenge.

If you have connections with a brass band for 50 years you are awarded a medal by the Wessex Brass Band Association. A few years ago I received my medal and I felt a complete idiot going up on stage to receive it. In fact my husband had to push me out of my seat! I had lots of support and I feel very proud whenever I pin it onto my uniform. Now I'm the oldest player in the band and the longest serving member.

A Chimney Sweep's Life - John Sansom

I was born in 1946 in Chard. My mother was not married but I know my father was an Italian prisoner of war who came from the camp up West Hill. The prisoners worked in the Cow and Gate factory and my father met my mother, and here I am. As her pregnancy became more obvious she was sent out of the way to Chard, as they did with women out of wedlock in those days. Within a week I was brought back to Wincanton and lived in Penn View with my mother, my grandmother and my Aunt Bessie.

My family in Wincanton goes back for generations. I know that my grandfather and his brother were put into the workhouse when they were kids because their mother couldn't look after them. Around that time there is documentary evidence of a Sansom stealing some bread and being sent off to Australia on a one way ticket. Perhaps he was my great grandfather.

My grandmother was a member of the Deane family and she worked as a daily housekeeper for the Maddox family at Southgate Farm, at the bottom of Southgate. It was still a farm when I went to school and I knew Fred Maddox and he told me that they all seemed to live on rice because it was the only thing my grandmother managed to cook properly! It was the Maddox family who donated large sums of money for the building of the Memorial Hall.

My grandmother Deane's father had four or five brothers and one of the brothers married a member of the Sly family who ran the White Horse Hotel. If you go in there you can see the name of Sly carved in one of the pillars. One of the Deane family married a Sly and that is how you have the name Deanesly Hall.

When I was about nine years old I was very friendly with an old man called Charley Meatyard who lived in Silver Street. He was a rabbit hunter and he would skin them and sell both the meat and the skins. The skinned rabbits were hung in the shed, the maggots ran through the body cleaning out the innards and then they would be washed out and sold. One day I asked him if he ever had any rabbits stolen. 'Yes, one,' he said, 'And I know where it went.' 'Well,' he said, 'I went down the allotments and there was Harry Mullins and Ernie Light and his wife down there. I said to him, you know what Harry? The cat died last night so I skinned it and hung it in the shed and when I got up this morning it had gone. Old Ernie and his Missus were up the hospital the next day because they thought they'd eaten the cat!'

When I was thirteen my mother and grandmother died in the same year. Auntie Bessie, who was single lived with us and didn't go out to work, and I had another aunt in the town, so I was well cared for. My mother hadn't been ill at all. She worked in the canteen at Cow and Gate, and wasn't in the house much, and when it was her lunchtime she walked up the town shopping for those who needed it. She never rested and would do anything for anybody. She collapsed in the front room with a thrombosis, they called the doctor and she was dead within an hour. I had an older cousin who was very down to earth and she said, 'You are born, you breathe, you die and once you are dead, you are dead.' I understood that.

I was friendly with an old lady called Mrs Reed who lived in Station Road in a little cottage and she had some cacti in her window. I said to her, 'Them cacti look nice.' She said to me, 'Do you like them,' and she showed me how to break a small bit off and put it into a new pot to grow. She had every shape and size under the sun. When she died she left me two hundred of them, and a greenhouse. My uncle, who lived a few houses further down the road helped me dismantle the greenhouse and we put it into his garden. I was staying there one night soon afterwards and was wakened by uncle who said, 'Better get out, me son, and come down the garden and give us a hand. The wind's blowing and the greenhouse is moving,' Me and he and my auntie stood there holding the greenhouse to stop the wind blowing it away. Glass was flying all over the place. It fell down in the end.

I left school at fifteen and went to work repairing roads for the Somerset County Council. I stayed there for seven years, then went lorry driving. But chimney sweeping is in my blood because my grandfather and his

John Sansom all set to kiss the bride

brother had been chimney sweeps in Wincanton. At that time there were quite a number of sweeps in the town. Tommy Jordan was the main man and he swept the chimney in the Grey Hound for Queen Victoria. Her wagon broke down on the road at Holton when a wheel came off, she was seven or eight years old at the time and she had to stay overnight in the town. That is how Tommy got, 'By Royal Appointment.' My grandfather on the Deane side repaired the wagon.

There was no official training for chimney sweeps and I was taken on by a nice old guy from Milborne Port. I met him in the road one day and I said to him, 'That looks an interesting job.' He said to me, 'Come out with me and I'll show you, because I want to retire.' That's how it came about. He had a real way with the posh ladies and would say to them, 'I've come to sweep your chimney.' They would say, 'Oh, Mr Fox, how nice to see you.' He replied, 'You look a well educated sort of lady, madam, I can tell that by looking at you. I'll tell you what, I bet you can't tell me what the twentieth letter of the alphabet is, can you?' Mr Fox would get on with laying all the cloths around the chimney and she would be out in the kitchen, her brain working like mad. She would come back in to us and say, 'Ah, Mr Fox, I think it is T.' He would reply, 'Thanks very much, no sugar.'

The best chimney I have ever swept was an eleventh century chimney in the Old House in Mere. The inglenook opening was around ten feet wide and at the side of it was a handle attached to a long metal rod which went all the way up the chimney. Across the top of the chimney was a large slab of stone which slid across the open chimney and when you turned the handle the stone moved over the opening closing off the chimney, which was a very clever idea for the summer months.

The lady of the house said to me one day, 'Do you go to weddings.' 'Weddings,' I said, 'I don't know much about that.' 'Oh, yes, it's lucky to have a chimney sweep at a wedding. I have a beautiful top hat in perfect condition which I can sell to you.' Off she went and brought into the room a beautiful leather hat box with the hat turned upside down inside it, which her father had bought years before for ten shillings and sixpence for the coachman to wear. That's how I came to dress up as a Victorian chimney sweep and you will often see me outside the church kissing the happy bride.

The render on the inside of a chimney is called polgin, and is a lime mortar which was trowelled on to the brickwork to prevent the smoke penetrating any cracks. If you use cement to line a chimney it cracks but lime mortar expands when the chimney gets hot and contracts when it cools down. But in the old days cow manure and horse hair was also used. The safest house you can get in the world is a thatch because the chimney is always built of brick and is polgin lined.

In Holbrook House Hotel, in the lounge, there is a very interesting fireplace which has a round fire back. This idea was said to be pinched from the Egyptians who designed it like that to draw better and it really works well. There are no corners for the smoke to get stuck in; it goes straight up the chimney.

Once I was asked to go and sweep all the chimneys in the empty Ireson House, up the top of the town. It was about eight o'clock at night in the wintertime. The house was very gloomy, the floorboards creaked, and it frightened the death out of me and I had to sweep all ten chimneys.

My brushes come from Barnsley in Yorkshire and are specially made for the chimney sweeping trade. I used to be able to buy Victorian designed brushes from a company in Mere and the bristles were properly drilled and tarred in. My brushes last me only two weeks and they are made out of polyurethane but they are not much good on Victorian chimneys. The top of a Victorian brush is a 2" woodstock and is designed to go round corners, modern brushes aren't. I have a couple of these old brushes which I can use if I need to.

Most of the soot I sweep goes into a landfill site. Soot has nitrogen in it and at one time farmers would buy tons of the stuff. But not many farmers and gardeners want it now. It is easier to go and buy large bags of fertiliser, and you can chuck it around without ending up black from head to foot. If you dig soot into your garden the slugs won't come in because they don't like it, it dries them out like salt. I have sold soot at times to the council who use it to mix with cement to tone down the colour.

If you have unseasoned wood that is the worst thing for causing chimney fires because it has sap in it and when you shut the wood-burner down the sap pickles and goes up as a vapour and lines the chimney. It is very highly inflammable so it's no good going out and cutting down a tree one day and burning it the next. If you have a chimney fire the best way to put it out is salt, just chuck in on; the vapour goes up the chimney and kills the fire. Mother used to have a block of salt by the fire, cut a slice off and scatter it all over the flames. But if you ever have a chimney fire you should always call the fire brigade – good advice given to me by Tommy Jordan all those years ago.